PATTERNS & BORDERS
NEEDLECRAFT SOURCE BOOK

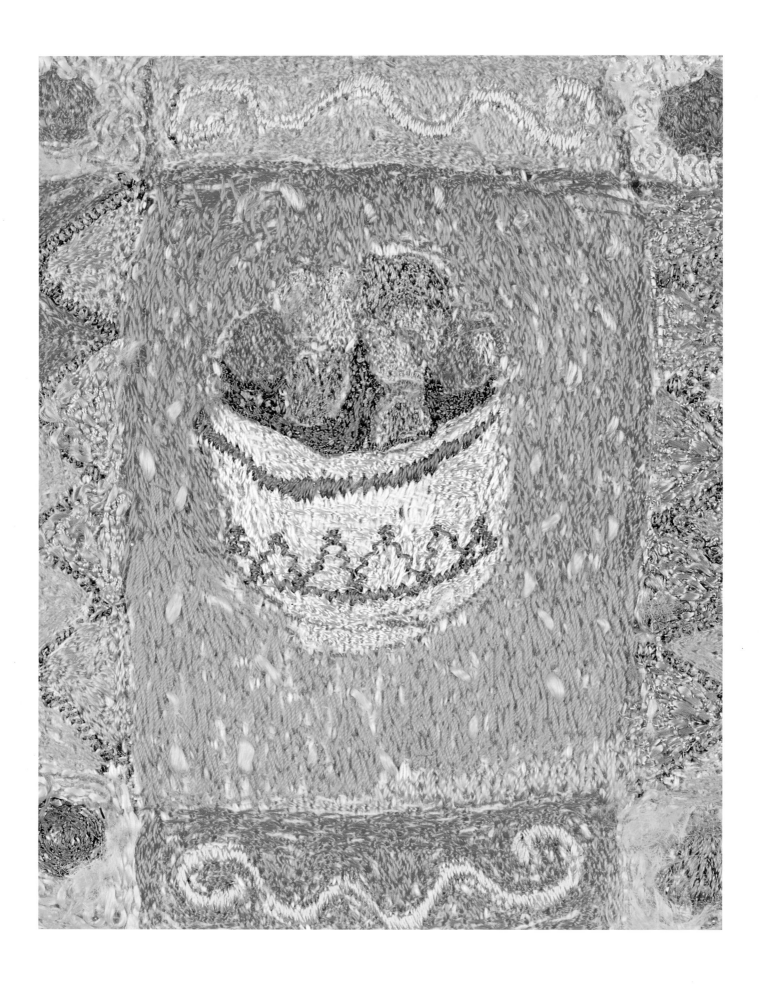

PATTERNS & BORDERS
NEEDLECRAFT SOURCE BOOK

GAIL LAWTHER

ANAYA PUBLISHERS LTD
LONDON

First published in Great Britain in 1992
by Anaya Publishers Ltd Strode House
44–50 Osnaburgh Street
London NW1 3ND

Editor: Patsy North
Designer: Sheila Volpe
Special photography: Jonathan Pollock/Di Lewis
Artwork: Tony Bellue, Michael Volpe, Julie Ward, Kate Simunek,
Lynette Mostaghimi

British Library Cataloguing in Publication Data
Lawther, Gail
Patterns and Borders Needlecraft Source Book
I. Title
746.44

ISBN 1-85470-115-0

Typeset by Servis Filmsetting Ltd, Manchester
Colour reproduction by J. Film Process, Singapore
Printed and bound in Singapore by Times Offset Ltd

CONTENTS

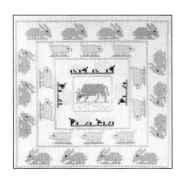

INTRODUCTION

Patterns and borders are some of the oldest forms of decoration. Patterns are found scratched on to prehistoric artefacts, stamped and carved on ancient examples of woodwork and metalwork, woven into textiles of all kinds, used to decorate items of religious significance, and incorporated into buildings, jewellery, furniture, clothing and everyday items of every culture in the world. The designs vary from extremely simple – for instance, a crude decoration carved with a stick around the rim of a prehistoric pot – to fabulously complex – for instance, the richly decorated layers of a Thai temple. Look around you wherever you go, and you'll see patterns everywhere, from the way that paving stones or bricks are laid out to the wiggly designs on tubes of toothpaste!

Whatever patterns or borders you discover, two features often unite the designs. First of all they usually consist of the same motif or design element repeated in different ways – perhaps a triangle placed at regular intervals along the edge of an archway, or two square patterns alternated in a chequerboard design. Secondly, the designs are often stylized, so natural objects such as leaves, flowers, birds or water might be depicted in a decorative way rather than a realistic one. Sometimes they are distorted in some way to fit into a regular shape; a flower may be drawn so that it fits exactly into a square, or a feather curved so that it fits into a triangle. Putting a motif into a regular shape makes it easier to build it up into a pattern, so this can be a handy trick when you're designing your own!

Patterns and borders are wonderful sources of inspiration for embroiderers. Every time I go on holiday, or away for a long weekend, I take a notebook and a pencil or pen and jot down little sketches of patterns I see. I've sketched designs from all kinds of sources, including the wallpaper in a pub, a set of railings outside a house, the pattern on a paper napkin, the distorted image of a building reflected in the windows of the building opposite, and the seat of a plastic chair. Once you start looking for patterns and borders, it's hard to stop. In this book, I want to show you what wonderful inspiration you can get for embroidery from the designs that surround us.

Each section takes its theme from a particular source of inspiration, such as geometric patterns, nursery motifs, or Christmas designs; in each section I have provided lots of drawings that can be used as a starting point for your own embroidery designs. Every design can be interpreted in an infinite variety of ways. If you are a beginner you can simply trace a design and stitch around the lines provided, and this will enable you to produce a well-finished piece of embroidery. If you are more experienced, you can use each basic pattern as a launching pad, interpreting it in needlepoint, appliqué, a mixture of embroidery and fabric painting, a starting point for machine embroidery or quilting, or any other technique or mixture of techniques that happens to take your fancy.

On each page of designs you will find plenty of ideas for taking the basic designs further. And, to whet your

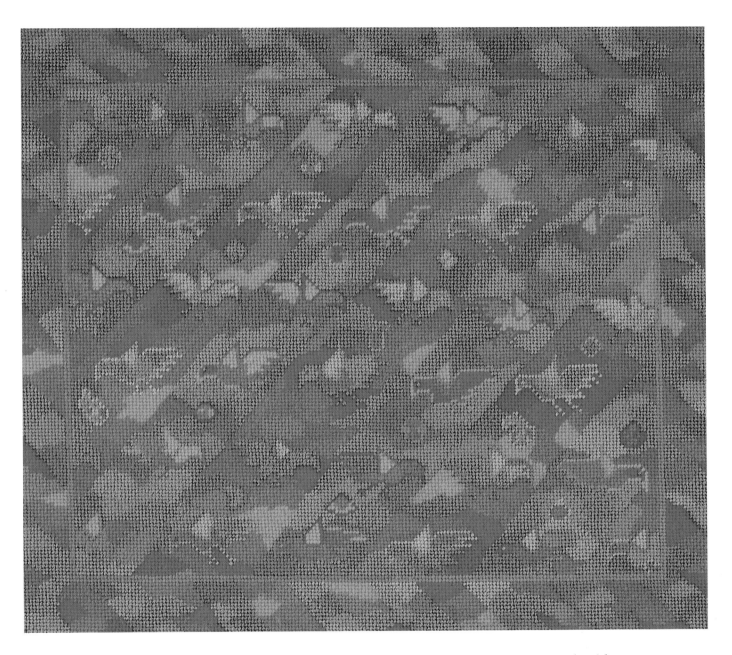

appetite and stimulate your own creativity still more, I've included a wonderful variety of inspirational pieces by different embroiderers, showing some of the many ways in which patterns and borders can be used to produce spectacular finished results. These embroideries cover a wide range of techniques, some traditional such as counted thread stitching, some illustrating contemporary embroidery methods. If you want to extend your knowledge of stitches and techniques, the section at the back of the book will give you some more ideas. I hope that you'll find the patterns and borders included here great fun to work with, and that you'll experiment with different ways of interpreting them to add your own individual touch.

Stylized birds fly across a sky of diagonal stripes, which break out into abstract shapes and diverse colour schemes.

Chapter 1

AROUND THE WORLD

Every country of the world, exotic or homely, has its own inspirational patterns and border designs – even your home country! Wherever you live or wherever you travel, look carefully at the things around you: interesting buildings, both old and new; clothes and fabrics; the decorations in shop windows or on greetings cards; flowers and trees; tiles, roofs and railings. The colours, textures, shapes and patterns will suggest designs that can be interpreted in embroidery, and fire up your own natural creativity.

If you travel abroad on holiday or business, take a sketch book and jot down ideas. You don't need to do complicated, accurate drawings; just make sure that you capture enough of the idea to be able to reproduce it when you get home. If you're in a hurry, just sketch in pencil or pen and make notes at the side about colours to jog your memory later.

Snapshots come into their own, too; they don't have to be great photographs – what you're looking for is a good reminder of shapes and designs, so go in close on details and decoration. Postcards are a good cheap source of inspiration, and the photography is usually very good quality; try and find shops where you can buy 'art' postcards rather than the usual views. Buildings – both inside and out – are often rich sources of inspiration with their different architectural styles; look at older ones for traditional details and designs, and modern ones for more contemporary or abstract ideas.

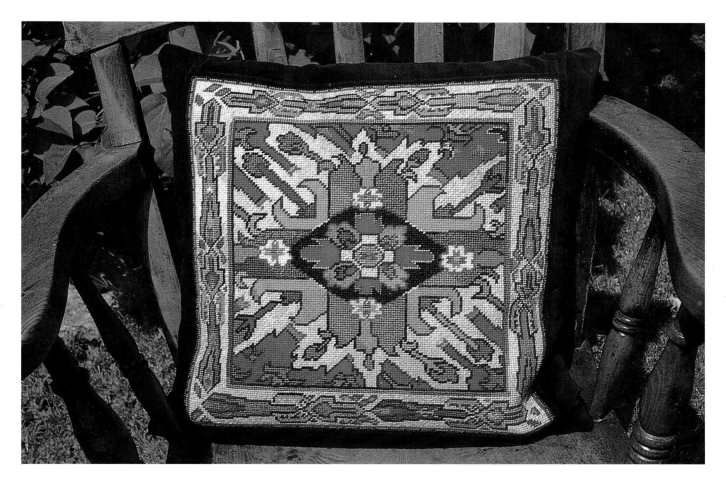

ABOVE *The design on this needlepoint cushion is based on the intricate patterning and rich colours of a traditional Persian carpet.*

LEFT *The striped blankets of the Plains Indians inspired this cross stitch pincushion, worked in several different shades of blue and yellow and counterpointed with metallic gold squares.*

If you don't travel much, browse through books in your local library. Travel guides are obvious places to hunt, but look too at books on hobbies, crafts, and technology; for instance, books on architecture, art, collecting different items, pastimes, cookery or fashion from different countries will give you all sorts of ideas. If you want information or ideas on a particular country, you can go to a travel agent and pick up a handful of brochures. All the brochures will be illustrated with views of the country concerned, and special interest holidays often feature plenty of arty photographs of events or sights such as festivals, particularly interesting or important buildings, traditional costumes, national dishes, and the local fauna and flora.

It is an interesting exercise to cut some of these pictures out, and to try rearranging them into a pattern that reflects different elements of a country's culture – by moving around bits of printed paper, or sections cut from snapshots, you may come up with ideas that wouldn't have occurred to you if you were just sketching. When you find an arrangement that you particularly like, do a quick sketch of it before you move the elements around again. Try taking a small design detail and repeating it in different patterns to see how variations look; make it into a straight or wavy or circular border, repeat it at different angles or inside various shapes, and try dotting it at random across a blank piece of paper. Once you've finalized a design, start thinking through ways in which you can interpret it in stitchery.

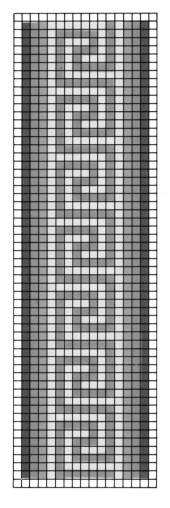

The border design used around these napkin rings is based on the maze-like Greek key pattern which, despite its name, is found in many different part of the world. These examples are embroidered in cross stitch, but the design would work equally well in any counted thread technique.

The swirling S-shaped pattern that frames these mythological Persian birds can be repeated vertically or horizontally, or worked as a mirror image. The birds are embroidered on linen using crewel wool; for a more contemporary look you could use bright stranded cottons, pearl cotton or coton à broder.

China, Japan, India and other Eastern countries have a heritage of exotic designs and patterns, many of which are very easily adapted for embroidery. All the designs here were inspired by the Orient, some of them based on stylized flowers and plants, others based on abstract patterns or calligraphic devices. To echo the oriental feel of the designs, work them in bright silks or exotic-looking metallic threads, perhaps on backgrounds of silks or satins. Many of these designs would lend themselves to couching or gold thread embroidery, perhaps to decorate a kimono-style silk wrap or a tasselled cushion.

The countries of Europe are many and varied, and each one has its own favourite patterns used in all kinds of decoration. This page features a tulip design – a favourite motif in Holland for needlework and painted decoration – which you could stitch in outline using stem stitch or chain stitch, or make more three-dimensional with satin stitch or long-and-short stitch outlined with back stitch. I've also included a counted thread border and an abstract design based on the intricate needlework patterns of Eastern European countries. The large circular drawing is based on a rose window in a French cathedral.

North and South America have very different traditions of needlework and other decorative crafts, from the complicated beadwork of the Plains Indians through to the highly stylized architectural patterns of the Aztecs and Incas. All the designs on this page are inspired by traditional designs from the Americas. The border at the top is based on one of the intricate traditional patterns worked in squares of coloured leather by the Alaskan people; you could interpret it in blocks of embroidery or appliqué, or perhaps in drawn thread work or beadwork. The feather design is a traditional Colonial American quilting pattern; you could use it for stitching a border around a patchwork quilt.

Africa is a diverse continent, and its patterns are as varied as its people and its countryside. The intricate interlocking patterns of North Africa can be seen on tiles, architecture, books, woodcarvings and stone-work – I've included two slightly simpler ones here, both of which are very versatile and would work well in appliqué and quilting as well as in embroidery. The cheerful tribal pattern round the edge could be extended for a dramatic picture or photograph frame, or you could stitch a border round the edge of a skirt.

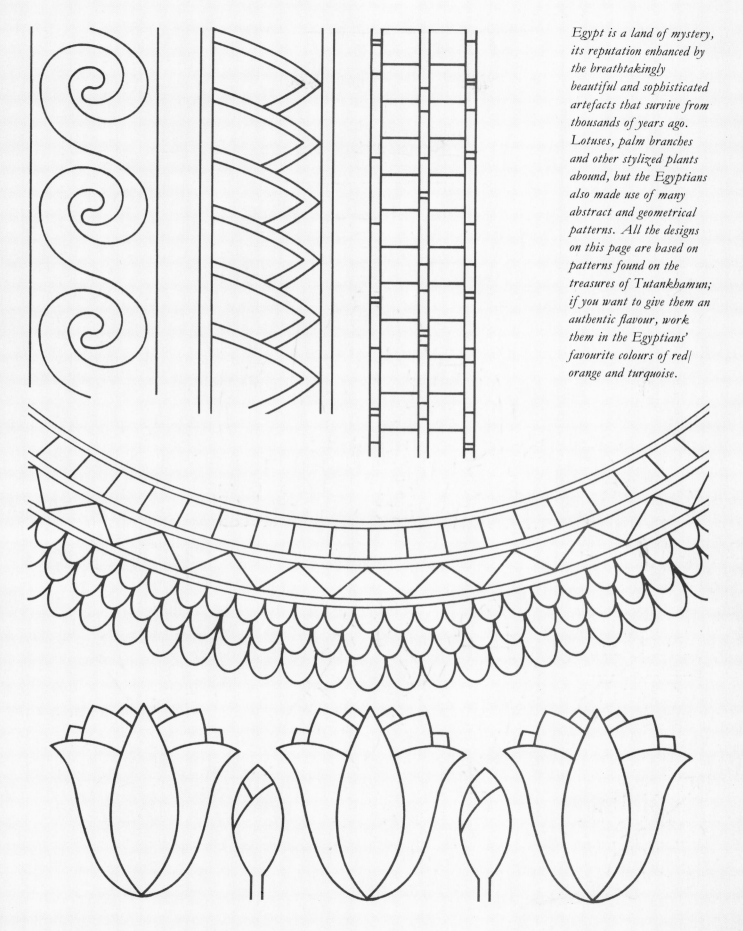

Egypt is a land of mystery, its reputation enhanced by the breathtakingly beautiful and sophisticated artefacts that survive from thousands of years ago. Lotuses, palm branches and other stylized plants abound, but the Egyptians also made use of many abstract and geometrical patterns. All the designs on this page are based on patterns found on the treasures of Tutankhamun; if you want to give them an authentic flavour, work them in the Egyptians' favourite colours of red/orange and turquoise.

Chapter 2

THE NATURAL WORLD

*Go for a walk in the countryside, and
you'll be surrounded by inspiration for
embroidery. Flowers, leaves and trees come
in all shapes and sizes, in myriad colours
and textures, from pale honeysuckle on
interweaving stems and bright cheerful
daffodils to the mellow tints of the turning
leaves. Add to this the sparkle of light on
a pond decorated by sapphire dragonflies,
the crisp bright tangy colours of summer
fruit, and quaint scenes of mother and baby
geese, and you have a world of ideas just
waiting to be translated into stitchery.*

Throughout the centuries, embroiderers have taken inspiration and ideas from the natural world around them. Flowers, leaves, fruit, trees, animals, birds, insects – these themes occur over and over again in ancient embroideries, but they still have plenty of power to inspire, and they are still just as popular today. Whether you want to stitch a traditional wreath of flowers or make a colourful contemporary machine embroidery inspired by the patterns on butterfly wings, you will find an inexhaustible supply of ideas all around you in the natural world.

PREVIOUS PAGE Flowers and leaves mingle here to form a needlepoint border and central panel; the subtle colours are set off well by the neutral background colour.

ABOVE AND RIGHT Varying your colour scheme can produce totally different effects with the same design, as you can see from this footstool and cushion, worked from the same chart. Stylized flowers and leaves alternate with squares to produce a repeat pattern.

Simply looking and drawing is one of the best ways to get ideas, of course, but sometimes, when you're out and about, you need to go in closer on some detail. Collect fallen leaves, pieces of bark, interesting bits of moss, and take them home to sketch from, or choose one particular theme such as flowers, trees or berries and see how many different shapes and colours you can track down. Magazines often have beautiful nature photographs and drawings; these can be good references for things that are hard to sketch *in situ*, such as birds and insects. Look in less likely magazine articles too; fashion photography is often done out of

doors, and you may find an inspirational background pattern of fallen leaves, ripples on water, sunsets or sunrises, mist and clouds.

Don't feel that you necessarily have to use realistic colours and shapes just because you are taking your inspiration from nature; many of the designs you are likely to draw from the world around you will lend themselves to stylization and to bold contemporary interpretations as well as more traditional ones. A good exercise for stretching your imagination is to take one design, for example a flower such as a rose, and try drawing it up in lots of different styles.

Satin stitch, feather stitch and French knots are among the stitches used in these pieces of whitework, which traditionally takes the motifs for its designs from the natural world.

Sketch it realistically, then stylize it in different ways – making it angular perhaps, or smoothing out all its irregularities, or working it into a stencil design. Then try putting the rose and its foliage into different shapes such as a circle, a triangle, a square, a diamond, a semicircle.

You can go on to make any of your designs into a repeat pattern or a border, trying different arrangements of the elements to see which ones work best. As you do this, you will probably begin to think of where you can use the shapes, and ways in which you can interpret them in embroidery. Try experimenting with alternative colourways; draw one design out roughly several times, and fill in the outlines with crayons or felt tip pens in different colour combinations. One way to broaden your approach is to pick a few skeins at random from a pile of coloured embroidery cottons; you may stumble across a new and dramatic colour combination.

RIGHT These quaint primitive birds have been embroidered in cheerful colours and surrounded by a background and border embellished with bright threads couched down in random patterns.

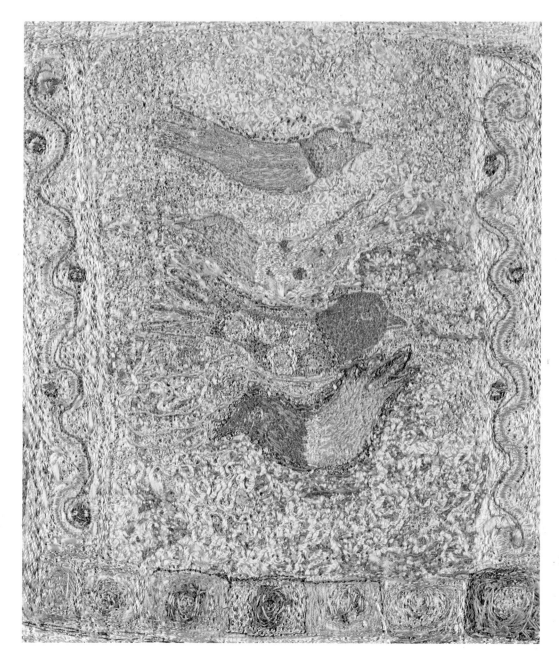

OPPOSITE The design for this panel of geraniums and a butterfly was taken from a Victorian tile; a simple geometric border pattern provides extra visual interest, and acts as a foil for the image inside.

RIGHT *Delicate little flowers are scattered across this needlepoint bag; you can easily extend the repeat pattern to cover a larger area such as a cushion. In the heart of each flower a gold bead provides a glistening centre.*

OPPOSITE *Embroidered lilies form the border for a striking place mat, worked here in long-and-short stitch. A single motif has been isolated and worked in a reverse colourway for the matching napkin.*

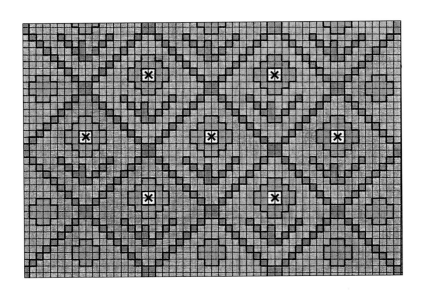

The natural world gives you wonderful opportunities to experiment with different textures. Collect photographs or real examples of items such as varied leaves or pieces of tree bark, and see how well you can capture their different textures. This is an ideal time to learn some new embroidery stitches; look through the section at the back of this book, or in stitch encylopaedias, and see which stitches might be suitable for reproducing particular effects. Try out random combinations of stitches and experiment with producing texture by placing the stitches at different angles, for instance by working irregular blocks of satin stitch in different directions on your backing fabric.

Intriguing textures can also be produced by varying the threads you use. Try experimental embroidery with some of the slubbed knitting yarns on the market; they can create interesting effects in stitches such as French knots and bullion knots, and if they are too thick to take through the fabric easily, you can try couching them down in regular or random patterns. Look outside the obvious world of embroidery threads and explore the possibilities of using materials from the natural world itself; raffia, straw, skeleton leaves, twigs, pieces of bark, grasses or strips of seaweed. Seeds or pieces of shell or polished stone can be used instead of beads, and will often provide you with a ready-made colour scheme straight from nature.

Flowers have probably inspired more embroidery designs throughout history than any other motif. They appear in the beautiful stylized silk embroideries of the East, the geometric counted thread designs of South America and Scandinavia, the quilting patterns and samplers of Britain and the United States, and in countless representational embroideries both old and new. On these pages I've included flower designs in as many different styles as possible for you to use as starting points for your own pieces in this ongoing tradition!

The large circular design is a traditional quilting medallion; you could work it in wadded quilting on a plain background, or perhaps try it in appliqué with coloured fabrics outlined in coloured stitching by hand or machine. The bluebells would make a delicate border embroidered up one side of a fabric photograph frame, or stitched in silk at an angle across the shoulder of a silk blouse. The tiny forget-me-nots are just asking to be stitched in French knots, with bullion knot or seeded leaves, while the oriental blossoms could decorate a kimono or bathrobe. The delicate honeysuckle blossoms would look wonderful in shaded silks or cottons, perhaps on an evening blouse.

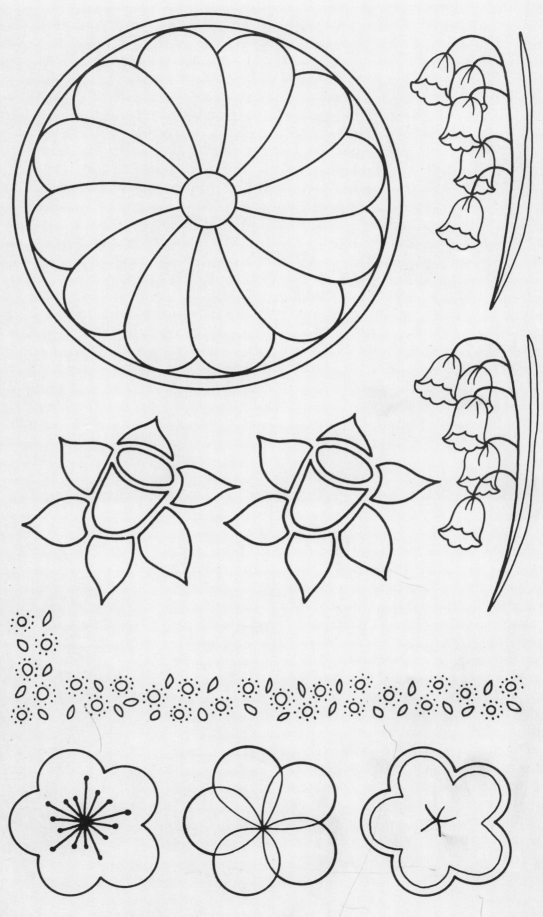

Leaves and trees are almost as varied and interesting in shape as flowers, although their colour range isn't quite as broad! These designs take a variety of approaches to the theme, ranging from realistic shapes, through stencilled and stained glass designs, to naïve trees perfect for decorating a child's bedroom curtains and cushions. The stained glass leaf border on this page could be worked as a very dramatic piece of appliqué, which would look wonderful round a large mirror in a light, contemporary room design. You could work the circular wreath of leaves as a tablecloth centrepiece in satin stitch, or much larger in outline round the edge of a tablecloth, maybe adding small beads as berries.

Mouthwatering fruits produce exciting mixtures of shapes and colours, as the cornucopia of designs on this page shows. Make the colours brighter than bright for a zingy modern approach, or subdue them for a more realistic depiction of the plum stencilled border or the grape cornerpiece. The grape design could be enlarged and stitched as cutwork in white or in colour for a fancy corner on a large tablecloth, perhaps with a single vine leaf in each of the other corners. The plum border would look lovely down the edges of cream curtains in a kitchen or living room, shaded in silks or stranded cottons, or stencilled with dappled fabric paints with surface embroidery.

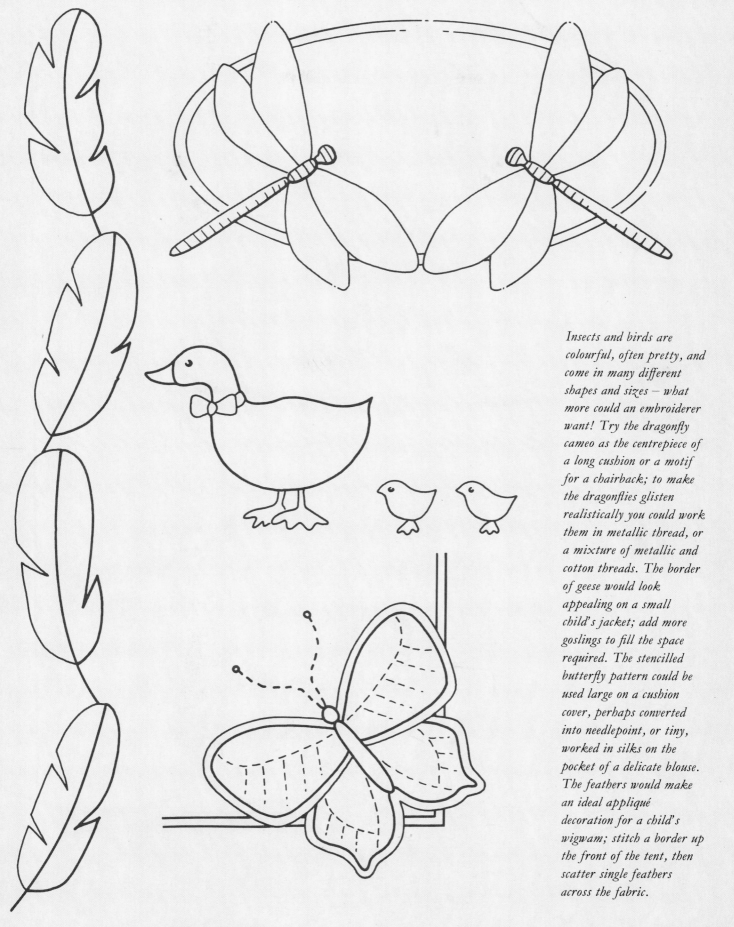

Insects and birds are colourful, often pretty, and come in many different shapes and sizes – what more could an embroiderer want! Try the dragonfly cameo as the centrepiece of a long cushion or a motif for a chairback; to make the dragonflies glisten realistically you could work them in metallic thread, or a mixture of metallic and cotton threads. The border of geese would look appealing on a small child's jacket; add more goslings to fill the space required. The stencilled butterfly pattern could be used large on a cushion cover, perhaps converted into needlepoint, or tiny, worked in silks on the pocket of a delicate blouse. The feathers would make an ideal appliqué decoration for a child's wigwam; stitch a border up the front of the tent, then scatter single feathers across the fabric.

33

Chapter 3

ABSTRACT DESIGNS

If you're looking for an embroidery design that gives you a wonderful opportunity to experiment with colour, texture and shape, then this is the section for you! Many patterns and borders can't be classified as anything representational, such as flowers or hearts or clouds; they are simply interesting shapes or motifs, arranged in an unusual way. They might be geometric, or regular, or almost totally random — abstract designs offer great scope to you as an embroiderer, whatever your favourite method of embroidery happens to be.

PREVIOUS PAGE *On this exuberant piece of embroidery, mythical birds and strange animals and fish mingle with all kinds of abstract patterns.*

RIGHT *A simple duck outline takes on an abstract appearance when overlapped in different directions.*

BELOW *Fish, snakes and birds are combined with symbolic motifs to create an abstract picture.*

You'll often find abstract design in unusual places; try looking at things like manhole covers and wrought iron, wooden logs and fences, textures woven into fabrics and stamped on plastics, patterns drawn round magazine advertisements and on book covers. Abstract patterns can be regular or random; you might find triangles, for instance, arranged in a very tight mathematical grid with regular repeats, or scattered unevenly and at different angles across a plain background. When you find an interesting pattern, make a quick scribble in your notebook, and keep a plastic folder for magazine cuttings that catch your eye.

When you're looking for inspiration, use these little scraps and scribbles as the starting point for your own unique designs. If you want a formal arrangement, see how separate pattern elements can be combined into a pleasing design. If you want a less structured pattern, try jotting down quick drawings at random across a blank sheet of paper, perhaps turning the paper to different angles as you draw, and clustering shapes more thickly in some areas than others. If you prefer one part of your final sketch to the rest, then draw a line round this section (or rub out the rest) and work it up into a finished design, repeating or enlarging it if necessary.

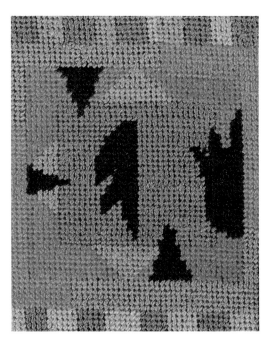

Vivid colours stitched side by side on this panel produce a fascinating study in tone. The black shapes provide a counterpoint for the brilliance of the other parts of the embroidery.

Stitch a bright case to guard your sunglasses on the beach. This design makes use of a deep border stitched in tent stitch, but you could use the same chart for cross stitch or other square stitches.

If you like working in counted thread techniques such as cross stitch, needlepoint, drawn thread work etc, it doesn't mean that your patterns necessarily have to be regular in structure. Simply draw your design out first freehand, then transfer it to a grid so that you can use the grid as a stitching chart. Some stitching shops sell clear acetate grids for this purpose; you put the grid of the chosen size over your original drawing, then trace on to the acetate with felt tip pens. If you can't obtain a clear grid, use graph paper over a light box, or thin squared paper so that you can still see the pattern.

Try using chain stitch for a varied texture in your embroidery – just three colours of thread are used for the simple abstract designs on this needlecase and pincushion.

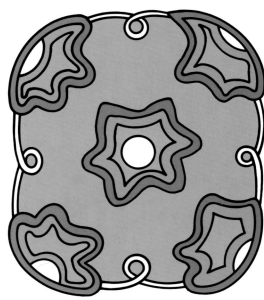

You can build extra drama into your abstract designs by introducing unusual textures and threads. Metallic threads are available in many different colours and thicknesses; sometimes finished embroideries can be quite overwhelming if they are stitched entirely in metallic threads, but sections here and there, or a metallic thread used in the needle alongside a cotton or silk thread, will catch the light intriguingly. Varying the texture of the embroidery can work well too; even if you are stitching a regular pattern in set colours, you can vary the stitches used in different parts for visual interest.

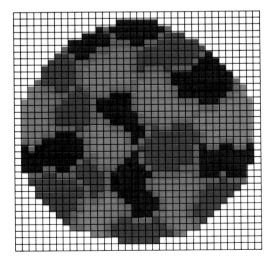

Royal colours of blue, purple, crimson and gold shimmer in the abstract design of this paperweight. The sheen of the viscose threads gives the embroidery an extra opulence, echoed by the imitation gold kid surrounding the design.

The ornate abstract shapes of Art Deco were the inspiration for all the designs shown here. Art Deco was the main influence in the decorative arts between the two World Wars, and perhaps as a reaction against the flowing and florid shapes of Art Nouveau, geometric designs became the vogue. Circles, squares, triangles, zigzags, stripes and diamonds came into their own, and certain stylized motifs such as lightning flashes and sunsets were incorporated into the decorations on everything from radiograms to jewellery, from textiles to whole buildings.

Bright colours are often associated with Art Deco designs, but the designers did use pastels and mid-tones too, and many of the patterns developed were designed to be worked in metalwork, so you could experiment with mixtures of gold, silver and bronze fabrics and threads as well as with other colours.

ABSTRACT DESIGNS

If you don't want a regular abstract design, let your imagination run riot as you interpret some of the ideas on these pages! The square and circular designs provide interesting ways of dividing a regular shape randomly; use them as a starting point for cushion designs, and fill in the shapes with your chosen method of embroidery. The rectangular frame opposite can be worked very dramatically in appliqué, using bright colours for the fabrics and black stitching for the lines where they join, or in complete contrast it could be worked in cross stitch or needlepoint as a sampler border in delicate pastels or gentle mid-tones of pearl cotton. The circular frame on this page would make a striking frame for a mirror, or a centrepiece for a circular table mat.

All the border designs can be extended indefinitely, so that you could work them on items such as the hem of a jacket or the edge of a tablecloth.

42

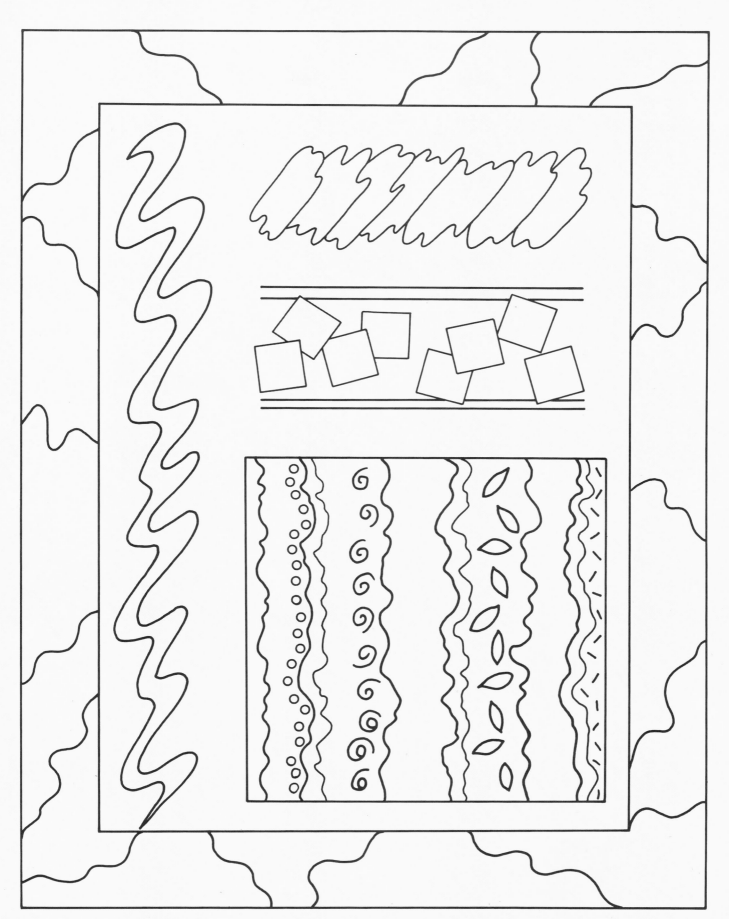

Chapter 4

VICTORIANA

Ornate flounces, ribbons and bows, the flowing lines of Art Nouveau, and the starker work of the Arts and Crafts movement; all these influences come across in the style of the Victorian era. Suddenly mass production meant that ordinary people could afford to have decorative items in their houses, not just useful and practical things, and decoration was what they filled their homes with — not a surface was left untouched! To our modern eyes Victorian design can seem overwhelming, but the era has provided a wealth of source material for embroiderers in the patterns and decoration that appeared everywhere.

PREVIOUS PAGE Typically ornate and full of fine detail, this Victorian panel was embroidered on to a printed silk ground.

RIGHT Stylized fruit, flowers and leaves intermingle on this Victorian table runner, worked in crewel work on a calico background. The brown and gold colouring is typical of later nineteenth century work.

OPPOSITE The highly elaborate Paisley border shown here has been embroidered in a variety of stitches and in subtly shaded colours, shown off well by the rich background colour of the tablecloth.

Although the Victorians tended to overdo their decoration, much of it was very attractive. Certain designers began to specialize in pattern design, and the craftsman William Morris was particularly involved in this area, working out theories that he then applied to carpets, furnishing textiles, tiles, porcelain, stained glass, furniture, architecture, wallpaper and book printing. We also owe to him and his family the revival of the craft of embroidery, which had all but died out as machines produced cheaply embroidered textiles; Morris and his designers developed what came to be called 'art needlework'.

Many designs from the Victorian era are still excellent sources of inspiration today. Look for books that feature Victorian tiles, textiles, furniture, clothes and crafts such as metalwork and marquetry. To cater for the continuing interest in Victoriana, whole magazines and books are devoted to so-called 'period living', and you will find them full of authentic details. Museums, too, are wonderful hunting grounds for Victorian artefacts.

RIGHT *This pretty fan pattern is stitched in gold on to black fabric and embellished with beads to make an elegant brooch. You could give the design a totally different look by working it in cutwork on the corners of a tablecloth or traycloth, or quilting it at the corners of a bedspread.*

OPPOSITE *Beads and dark velvet give a Victorian flavour to this evening bag, worked in rich blue and purple needlepoint. You could adapt the design to other colour schemes — choose one from an evening dress of your own.*

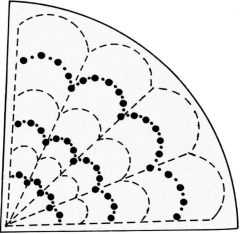

Opulence characterizes a great deal of Victorian design, and often their embroideries were embellished further with beads, velvets, sequins, jewels and thick metallic threads. Crazy patchwork was a passion to the Victorians; they would stitch together random sections of rich fabrics, often velvets or brocades, then cover the joins with embroidery, sometimes adding yet more embroidery or beadwork to the patches in different designs.

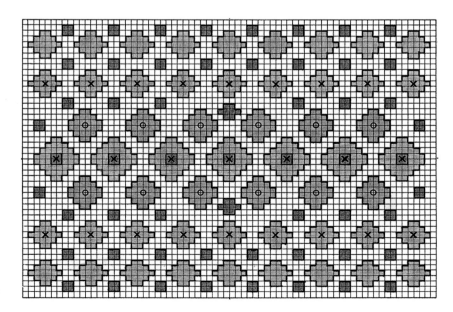

You can get an authentic Victorian feel into your embroidery by working with beads and sequins; if you are using a counted thread technique such as cross stitch, or any kind of needlepoint, you can insert a bead on each stitch in the same colour as the thread you are using, and this will produce a textured embroidery – or just use beads on one area. Vary your embroidery still more by hunting around for different styles of beads, or by using beads from old necklaces and belts of the time. If you are working free-style embroidery, add beads or purls (small snips of metal) on accents such as the stamens of flowers, the eyes or wings of insects, the veins of leaves or the outlines of borders or other patterns.

The Victorians loved swirling, interlocking, very ornate shapes, often based on stylized plant forms but sometimes semi-abstract. Foreign travel was becoming increasingly popular with the educated classes, and as leisured people travelled they jotted down ideas in their sketch books and also brought back exotic fabrics, which added extra ornamentation to a style that was already elaborate. Some of the designs here, based on Victorian items such as tiles and architectural borders, show this love of ornate interweaving forms; try interpreting them in mixtures of coloured and metallic threads, heavily textured, for an authentic Victorian look. Paisley patterns were developed during the Victorian era; the Paisley pattern on this page could be used in a repeat pattern or singly.

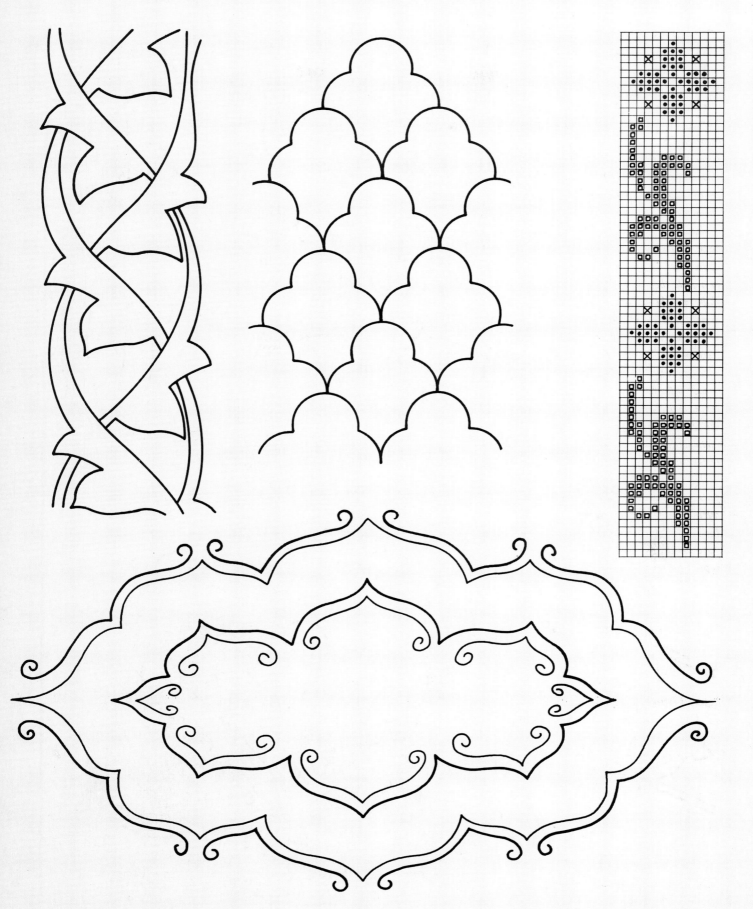

Frills and flounces abound in Victorian decoration, often giving the impression of an overwhelming sentimentality; as a result, Victorian designs are full of ribbons and bows, hearts and crowns, pretty little angels and cherubs. The designs on these pages have all been inspired by the pretty side of Victoriana, and you can use them to decorate your own pretty needlecraft projects. The ribbon-and-bow border and circular frame work well on wedding cards and samplers, and the border would also be very effective worked along the hem of a wedding dress. The cornerpieces opposite are ideal for cutwork or for satin stitch embroidery; you could stitch them at the corners of traycloths or other items of table linen.

The sinuous curves of Art Nouveau are unmistakable; it is notsurprising that its enemies referred to it variously as tapeworm style or noodle style! Art Nouveau took its lines from nature, particularly the flowing lines of plants, water and women's hair, which were made to curve and intertwine elaborately. Oriental motifs such as water-lilies and stylized clouds were very popular, and the peacock in particular was idolized as the most exotic of birds; its feathers appear over and over again in Art Nouveau decoration, so I have included a peacock-feather frame here. The style of the Glasgow School of Art was more geometric and stark, but no less influential; some of the designs on these pages are based on their simple but opulent lines.

Chapter 5

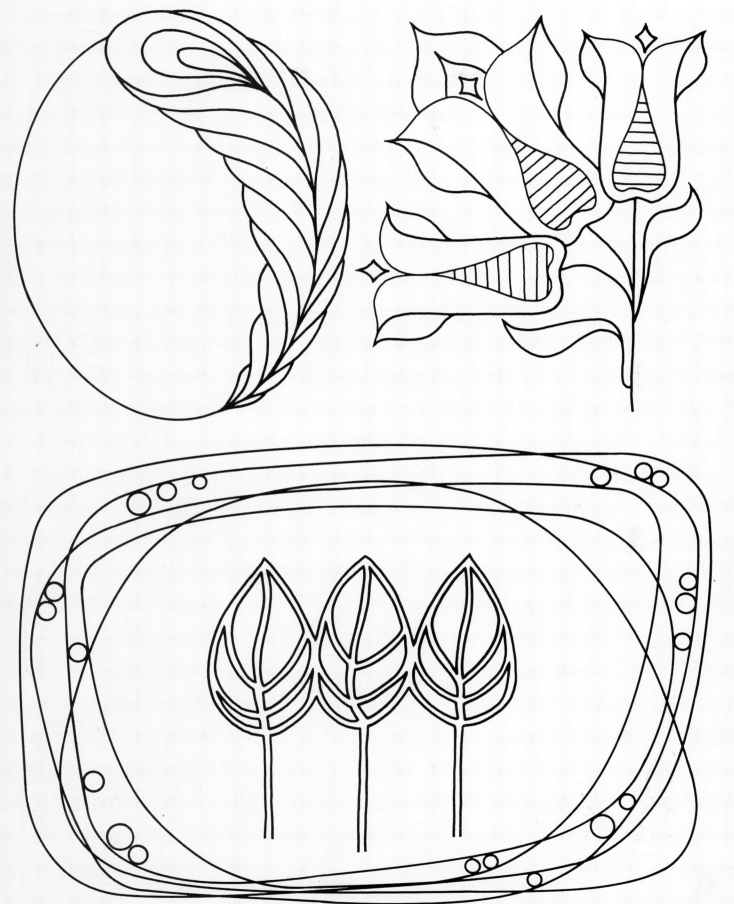

SEASONS

Spring, summer, autumn and winter: their names evoke all kinds of images in our minds. Spring flowers in delicate shades; a blazing summer day of clear cloudless skies; the crunch of autumn leaves underfoot; winter mornings crisp with the promise of frost and snow. Everyone has their favourite season; whichever it is, you should find inspiration for your embroidery in these pages of seasonal designs.

Every season has its classic images — bonfires in autumn, snowmen in winter, beach scenes in summer and so on. And there's nothing wrong with these evocative scenes, but it's worth digging a bit deeper, too, for some less obvious images. For instance, perhaps your favourite season is autumn. Try and pinpoint what it is that you particularly like about it. The temperature? The scents on the air? Harvest festivals, with their profusion of fruits and vegetables in different colours and textures? The feeling that a sharp winter is just around the corner? The patterns of the trees or the textures of country paths as you walk along them? Then see if you can come up with images, realistic or abstract, that sum up some of those sensations.

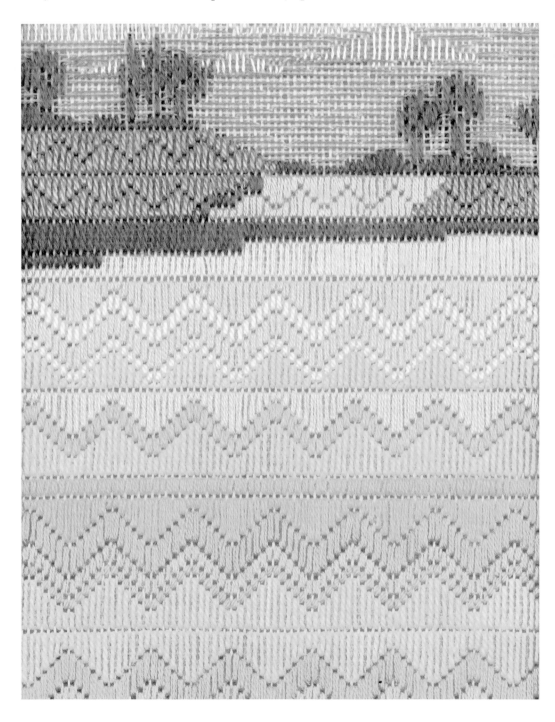

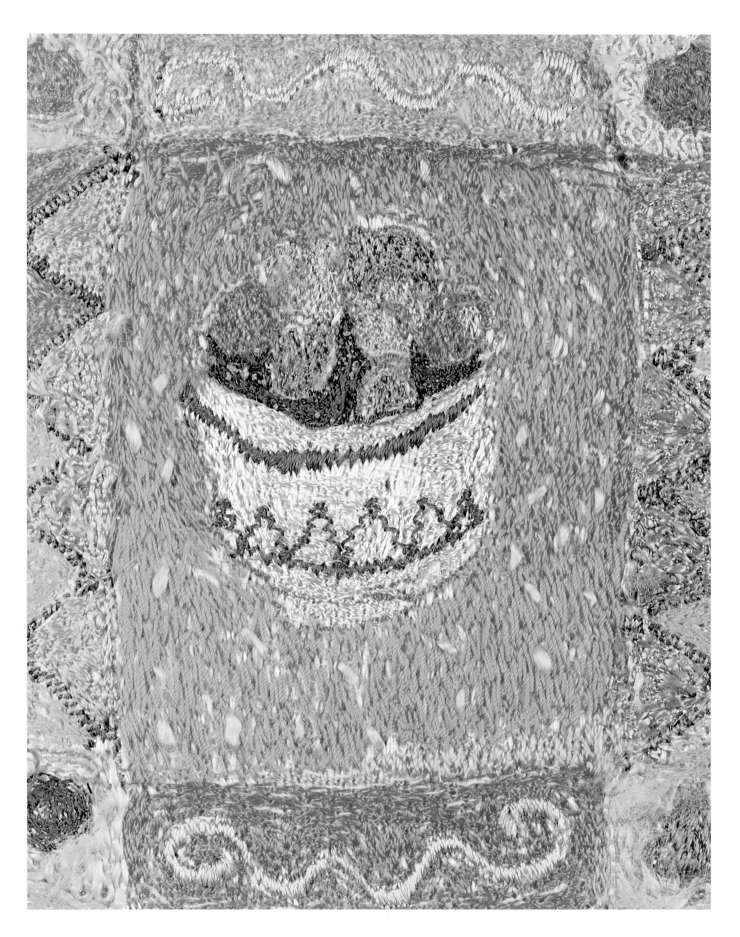

Using images from magazines can help you to analyse your response to different seasons. Leaf through lots of old colour magazines and tear out any bits – whole images or tiny details, or even words – that remind you of each of the seasons. Put the pieces into four separate piles, one for each season. Then do the same with colours: make four collections of seasonal colours and textures, using odd scraps of fabrics, threads, wools, pieces from colour charts, more bits torn from magazines, scraps of lace, pieces of textured paper etc. Pick one of the seasons, and see what ideas you have come up with relating to it; the bits and pieces you have collected will probably give you lots of ideas for evocative seasonal embroideries of different kinds.

Autumnal ears of corn decorate the sides of this tent stitch tissue box cover. The same motif would make an effective repeat pattern in cross stitch along the edges of a table runner or around a canvas belt.

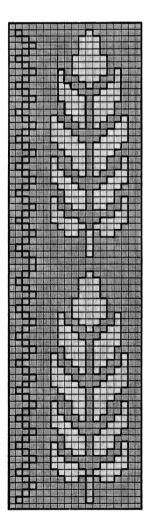

One way that you can enrich your embroideries is by incorporating 'found objects' into your designs; the seasons often seem particularly appropriate themes for this idea. For instance, in an embroidery on the theme of autumn you could include real ears of corn, pieces of bark, seed-heads, real leaves, dried berries and bits of twig. A stitched panel worked to remind you of a perfect summer holiday could include pebbles from the beach, feathers from local birds, dried starfish, or shells that have been pierced so that they can be stitched to the background. If you find a particularly beautiful item that would be perfect as the centrepiece for an embroidery, for instance, an exotic piece of abalone shell or mother-of-pearl, then you could take the colours and textures for the rest of your embroidery from those you see in your found object.

Succulent red strawberries are enriched in this needlepoint piece by gold 'seeds' stitched into the design. Use just a few repeats of the design, as here, or extend it for a cushion, a curtain tie-back or an exclusive waistcoat.

Spring is synonymous with new life; flowers and leaves peep through the earth after a long hibernation, butterflies emerge from chrysalises, and baby chicks emerge from eggs! Spring colours are often pastels or mid-shades, bathed in a subtle light; no one seems to want to be reminded of the short dark days of winter. Use the circular borders here to stitch pretty table linen to brighten up the days, or to frame a favourite photograph – perhaps a spring wedding. The decorated eggs are ideal as a border for a celebration Easter tablecloth, or they can be used singly or in small groups on Easter cards. The butterflies can be used in any grouping, perhaps stitched in mid-pastels across a blouse.

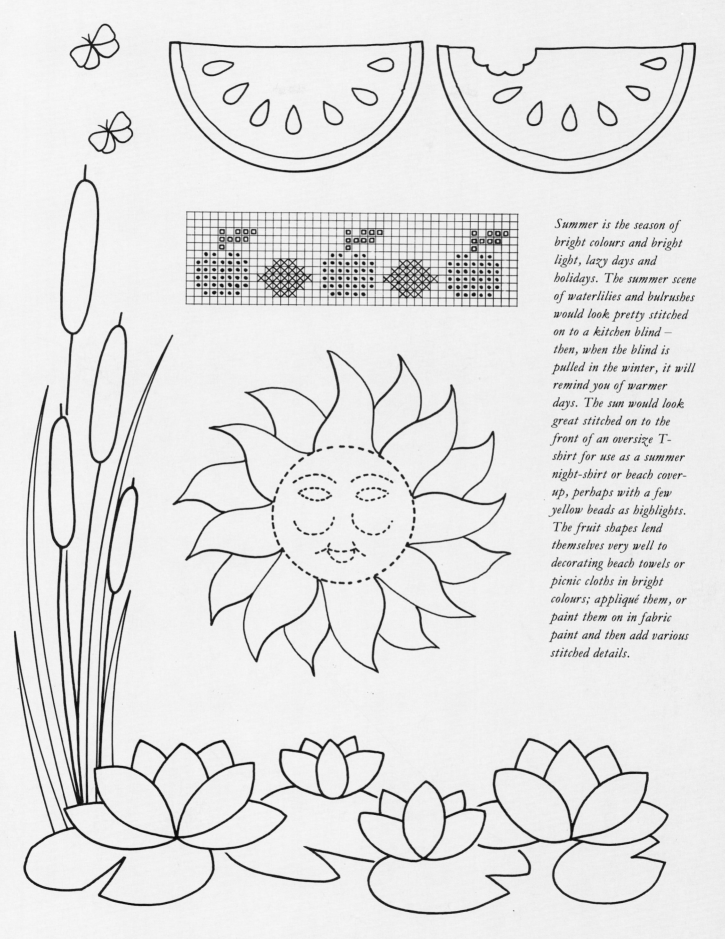

Summer is the season of bright colours and bright light, lazy days and holidays. The summer scene of waterlilies and bulrushes would look pretty stitched on to a kitchen blind — then, when the blind is pulled in the winter, it will remind you of warmer days. The sun would look great stitched on to the front of an oversize T-shirt for use as a summer night-shirt or beach cover-up, perhaps with a few yellow beads as highlights. The fruit shapes lend themselves very well to decorating beach towels or picnic cloths in bright colours; appliqué them, or paint them on in fabric paint and then add various stitched details.

Autumn leaves are almost a cliché, but there's still a fascination in their seemingly endless variety of shapes, colours and textures. The border above combines stylized oak leaves and acorns, and would look very pretty worked round the edge of a large warm scarf for windy autumn walks. Harvest festival is always a visual feast, as the colours of the different fruits and vegetables contrast with the rough textures of grain and loaves; use some of the images in the border at the top of the page, or the circle of corn ears and poppies, to stitch a church banner or a centrepiece for your own home celebration. If you're working on a large scale, you could appliqué the main shapes before embroidering details.

Winter conjures up images of snuggling up warmly while the elements do their worst! Use the umbrella or snowman borders to decorate a child's raincoat; you can extend the snow above the snowman as far as you like. For cold mornings, embroider a couple of steaming mugs on to the front of a warm dressing gown; again, you can extend the swirls of steam, stitching them in an outline stitch such as back stitch or chain stitch. Snowflakes always look pretty — these three charts are very versatile and could be used for an all-over winter picture, or singly on Christmas cards.

Chapter 6

GEOMETRICS

Lines, squares, circles, triangles, diamonds, stripes — many of the different patterns and borders used throughout history have been based on combinations of these simple geometric elements. You can use them in very plain designs, or combine them into patterns of the greatest complexity; on these pages you'll find lots of ideas to start you off.

PREVIOUS PAGE This needlepoint panel uses almost tribal symbols. The design is given extra visual interest by varying the colour combinations across the canvas.

RIGHT This little panel shows the effect of changing the colourway across a basic repeat pattern; each motif formed by a circle and triangle looks completely different from its neighbours.

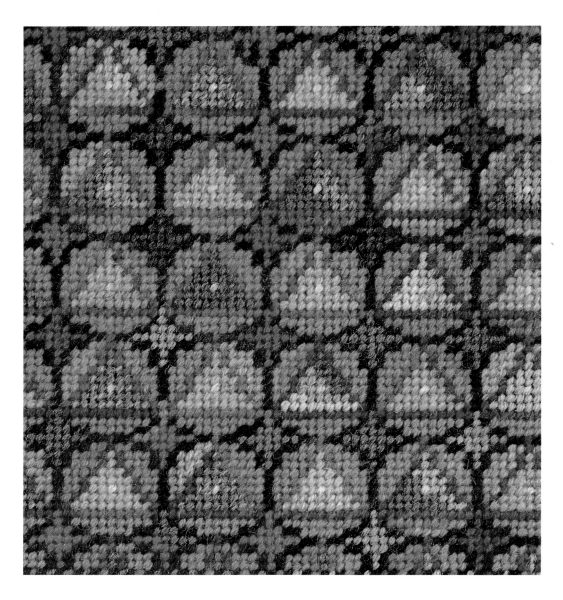

Geometric designs can be very simple and still be effective if you choose strong shapes for your design, as you can see from this small needlepoint panel.

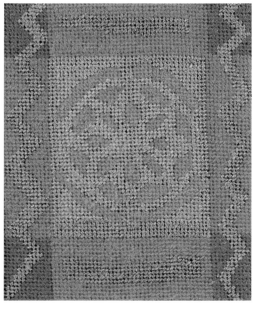

The ways of using, combining and varying geometric shapes for embroidery are infinite. Starting off with only a grid pattern of squares, just think of all the different ways that you can alter colour schemes and their arrangement, from a basic chequerboard design in two colours through to a complex repeat pattern using twenty or thirty colours. Then think of the ways in which you can alter the squares themselves – varying their sizes, overlapping them, turning some at an angle, positioning them at random on a background, working them into solid shapes to make a pattern or to represent a stylized animal or flower, or a letter of

the alphabet. And we're still only looking at one shape! Add triangles, diamonds, cones, pyramids, rectangles, circles, parallelograms, ellipses and stripes, plus all the different ways in which they can be combined, and you have a resources library that you'll never exhaust.

Even with a simple geometric pattern, there are numerous ways in which you can vary it by the threads, fabrics, stitches and techniques that you choose. A basic chequered border of squares could be given several totally different treatments; for instance, stitched in needlepoint in black and white, worked in blocks of pastel satin stitch, filled with Jacobean crewel work in rich wools, or interpreted in metal thread embroidery.

The bright geometric patterns of African beadwork have been translated here into two colourful but very simple cushion designs in giant cross stitch. The designs would work well small, too, perhaps stitched very tiny as brooches.

This striking cushion design uses cushion stitch — squares of diagonal satin stitch worked on to canvas. The squares are worked in blocks of four of the same colour and are finished off with back stitch.

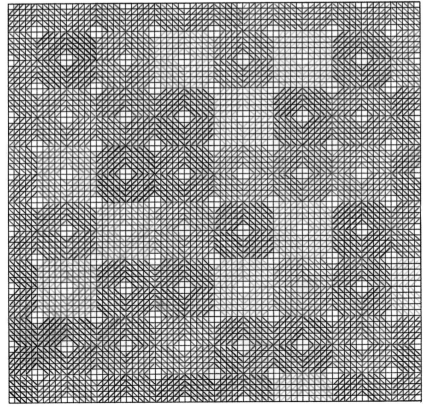

Geometric patterns crop up everywhere, from patterns on kitchen flooring to the shapes made by a coiled telephone wire. When a pattern catches your eye, jot it down in your notebook before you forget it, even if it seems humdrum; you may be able to transform it with embroidery. Computers are a good source of geometric designs — not just sophisticated ones that actually produce charts for knitting or needlework, but more basic ones which often have border patterns or little symbols that make good starting points for embroidery designs. Architecture, too, can provide plenty of inspiration for geometric patterning, especially the uncluttered symmetry of modern buildings. A row of skyscrapers silhouetted against the skyline, with their regular patterns of windows, can spark off all kinds of interesting ideas.

The subtle geometric design for this pincushion makes use of circles, dots and diamonds in three colours, worked in tent stitch using tapestry wool.

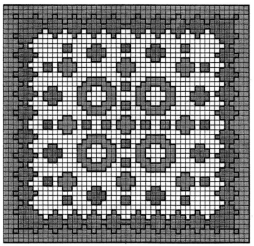

Not all geometric designs are counted thread designs, by any means, but you may want to translate some of the designs here or some of your own freehand ones into charts for cross stitch or needlepoint. This can be done with an acetate grid, or by tracing on to graph paper, but one way to produce a full-colour chart divided into squares is by using colour photocopying. Most colour photocopiers offer a service which enables you to have your image broken down into different coloured squares, or pixellated.

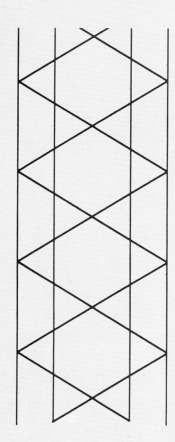

Patchwork patterns are virtually always geometric, and they translate very well into other types of stitchery. Look through pattern books in your library or in specialist bookshops, and you may well find ideas that stimulate your imagination. All the designs on this page are based on patchwork patterns; because they are so regular, most of them adapt very well to counted thread work. The square pattern is one of many variations on a basic patchwork star; many traditional block designs are based on stars, and they look very effective translated into embroidery.

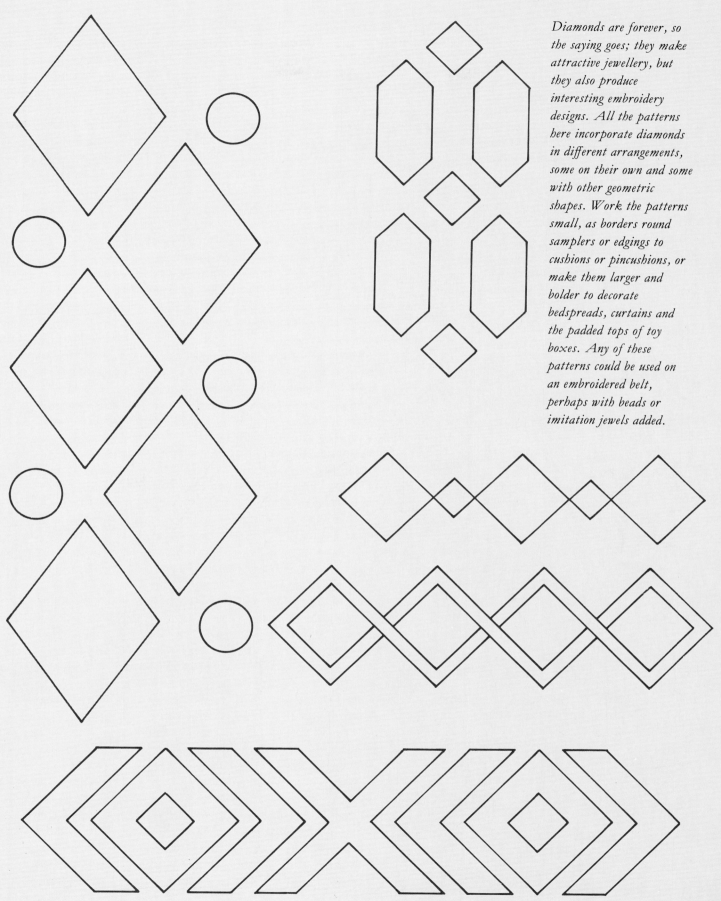

Diamonds are forever, so the saying goes; they make attractive jewellery, but they also produce interesting embroidery designs. All the patterns here incorporate diamonds in different arrangements, some on their own and some with other geometric shapes. Work the patterns small, as borders round samplers or edgings to cushions or pincushions, or make them larger and bolder to decorate bedspreads, curtains and the padded tops of toy boxes. Any of these patterns could be used on an embroidered belt, perhaps with beads or imitation jewels added.

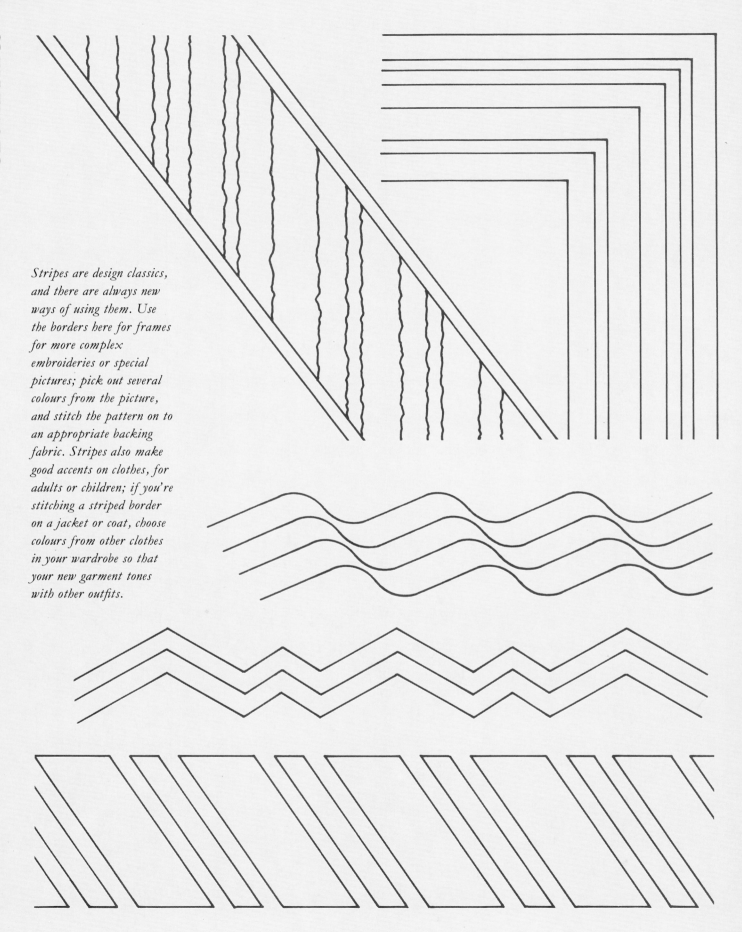

Stripes are design classics, and there are always new ways of using them. Use the borders here for frames for more complex embroideries or special pictures; pick out several colours from the picture, and stitch the pattern on to an appropriate backing fabric. Stripes also make good accents on clothes, for adults or children; if you're stitching a striped border on a jacket or coat, choose colours from other clothes in your wardrobe so that your new garment tones with other outfits.

Sashiko quilting is a Japanese needlecraft technique that involves producing texture on a background fabric by working a long running stitch in geometric patterns. The patterns can be very complex, but many of them are relatively simple; the dramatic effect comes from the combinations of colours and patterns and the rich threads used. All the geometric designs on this page are Sashiko patterns; you can use them on small items, or extend them to cover whole bed quilts. Don't feel that you have to use them as quilting patterns, though; try interpreting them in needlepoint, surface embroidery, drawn thread work and machine embroidery, or couch the designs in thick gold threads on to a coloured silk or satin background.

75

GEOMETRICS

Many geometric designs are not abstract, but are based on stylized forms of ordinary objects such as flowers, leaves, stars, animals, feathers, fans, birds or people; the designs on this page are geometric patterns in this tradition. Eight-petalled flowers like the ones below are found in the embroidery heritage of many different countries, often worked in cross stitch and sometimes in beadwork – use them in a border, or scatter them singly in different sizes across a peasant blouse or an evenweave cushion. The stylized shell shape would look effective as a satin bed-cushion, perhaps quilted with machine satin stitch and scattered with little shell or pearl beads.

Surprisingly, the humble square is the basic inspiration behind many complex geometric patterns. Many countries have developed their own characteristic designs, some of them using the squares and their derivatives so that they overlap or interlock, and others so that they are set at different angles. The designs on this page are all based on combinations of squares; this makes them very easy to interpret in counted thread techniques, but they can be used just as effectively for free-style embroidery. Try using them for patchwork, quilting and appliqué, too, embellished with different embroidery stitches.

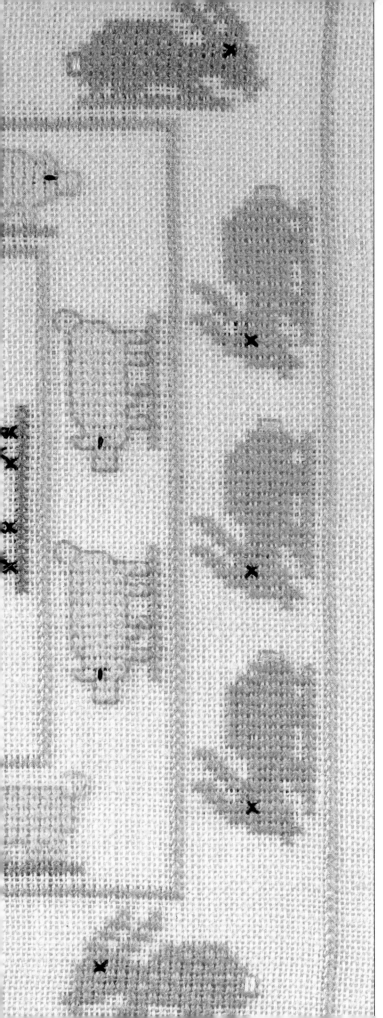

Chapter 7

NURSERY DESIGNS

Children love to be surrounded by bright, bold shapes in clear colours, and there are lots of ways that you can use the designs in this section to create fun items for them. Favourite toys such as building blocks, jigsaw puzzles, balloons and trains can be transformed into friezes for duvet covers or frames for samplers. Pastimes that every child enjoys — like kite flying and eating ice cream — are echoed in borders for holiday clothes or beach towels, and patterns of cut-out dolls and pawprints will remind them of a faithful companion.

PREVIOUS PAGE *Stylized farm animals graze their way happily round this square panel; you could use any simple motif in a square design in this way.*

Nursery designs are easy to draw yourself, as they don't need to be sophisticated – in fact, the simpler the shapes are, the more easily the child will recognize them. Stylized toys, teddies, animals and shapes from the everyday world can be incorporated into all kinds of embroidery for your baby or toddler, and older children will like having a special piece of stitchery that has been done exclusively for them. You'll find inspiration from all kinds of children's goods; everything from high chairs to baby wipes tends to be decorated with little motifs that catch a child's attention. Try drawing your own versions of some of the shapes you

find on toy boxes or food packets; once you're happy with your drawing, make borders by repeating the motif, perhaps arranging the repeats at regular intervals or alternating mirror images.

Don't worry about putting sophisticated shading or colouring on to your designs, or even about making your shapes ultra-realistic; look through a selection of children's books, and you'll see that the shapes are very simple and clear, and usually coloured in flat, bright tones. This will make your task much easier, and may give you the confidence to try more ambitious ideas – for instance, drawing a scene of Noah's ark and all the animals.

RIGHT *For this photograph frame, numerous different nursery shapes have been combined and stitched in bright colours. The angles of the toys and the way that they overlap the central panel break up the rectangular lines of the frame attractively.*

OPPOSITE *Eggs in egg-cups make very satisfying shapes that are easy to stitch. On this panel each egg-cup is different, from the traditional duck to a tartan version!*

A sampler is a lovely way to welcome a new baby, and it is appreciated even more if you've designed it yourself! Stitch the baby's name and date of birth in a simple cross stitch alphabet, and surround it with one of these charming border designs.

You can use any colours on nursery patterns and borders, but you'll probably find that your embroidery ties in best with the rest of your child's belongings if you work it either in pastels or in bright colours. If you're stitching something to decorate a child's room, look around the room first to see if there is a ready-made colour scheme that you can pick up, for instance in the curtains or bed-cover. If you're decorating an item of clothing,

see what other clothes might be worn with it and choose your coloured threads accordingly. Maybe you could let your child pick out his or her own design and colour scheme; that way it seems extra-personal. You might find, too, that some of the shapes are simple enough for your child to help with the stitching in places – or you could pick out a single motif and draw it up large for your child to embroider in easy stitches and thick threads.

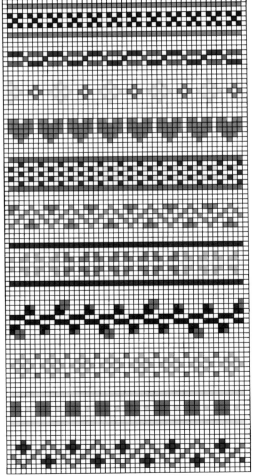

Gingham looks pretty in any nursery, and is ideal for cross stitch designs because you can place the stitches very accurately. Use the charts to stitch borders, a symmetrical design or randomly placed flowers on to a gingham cot quilt for your baby.

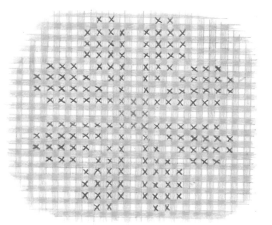

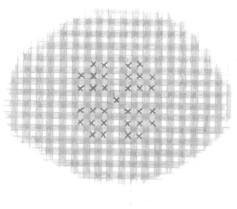

All the children's borders here have lots of different applications. Use them small on nursery samplers, birth congratulation cards, pictures for a child's bedroom or to decorate a T-shirt or skirt, or blow them up large and appliqué them to playmats, duvet covers, toy bags, floor cushions or activity pictures. The train can be made so that each carriage is a pocket for a toy; appliqué bright felt shapes by machine on to a sturdy background. The clouds and rainbow would look very pretty as a frame for a picture or mirror, worked in cross stitch or satin stitch, or you could draw the design larger and use it for a quilt.

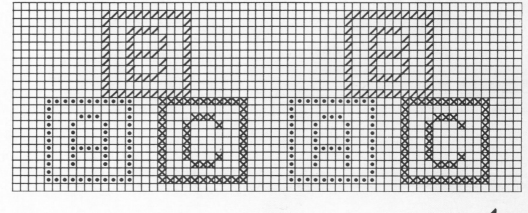

84

Favourite insects make their appearances on this page; the butterfly, bee and ladybird borders have many uses, and the borders can be extended to make them as long as you want. Use one round the edge of a little girl's skirt or across a pair of dungarees; if you don't feel confident about stitching the insects themselves, you could buy a few novelty buttons in the right shape and just stitch the wiggly line. The row of paper doll shapes can be extended as you wish, and could be used across a picture, perhaps with the child's name underneath. If your family has a cat or dog, your child might enjoy a floor cushion with a pattern of pawprints outlined or appliquéd across it. Balloons and kites remind us of happy days out; use them to decorate a set of warm outdoor clothes, perhaps an anorak and jeans.

The alphabet chart is very versatile. Translate it into cross stitch and you have a simple sampler, or use the chart much bigger as the pattern for an appliqué cot quilt or a large cross-stitch rug for the nursery floor.

Chapter 8

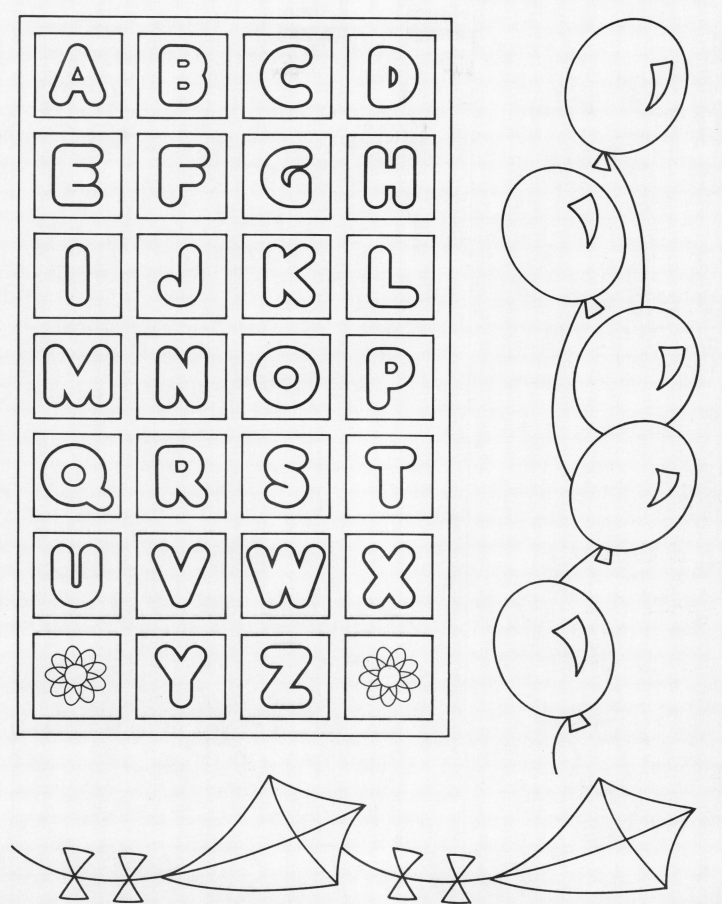

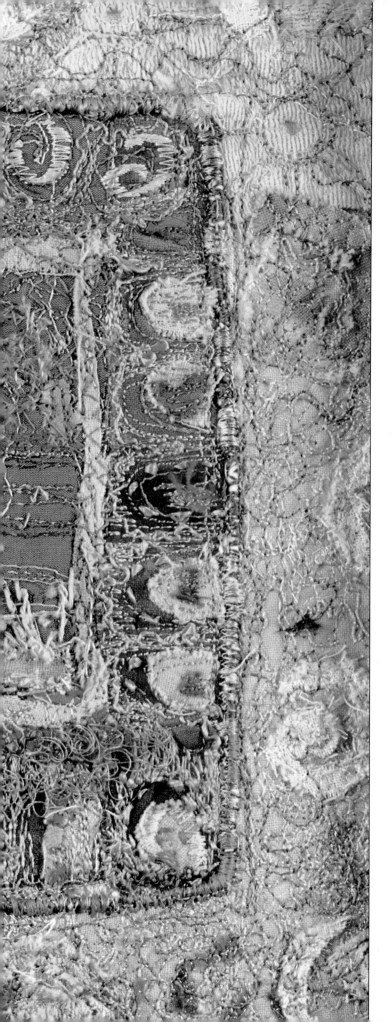

HOLIDAYS

What comes into your mind when you think of holidays? Sun, sand, sea and shells on a palm-fringed shore? Waves crashing against a lonely windswept headland? Sailing the high seas? Or perhaps something closer to home: a family holiday with a trip to the circus, pauses for ice cream, and expeditions to amusement parks and funfairs. In this part of the book, you'll find a selection of designs that capture the holiday mood.

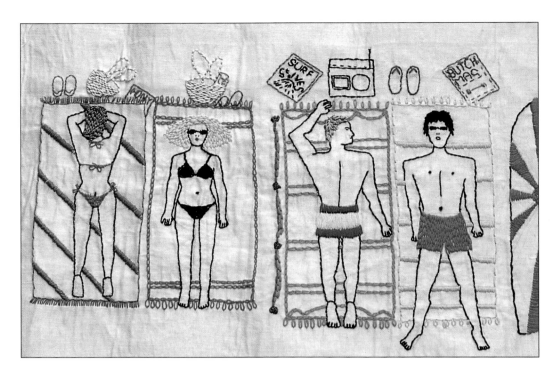

Holidays are both a source of inspiration for embroidery, and a good excuse to do something special in the way of stitchery. It often adds to the excitement and anticipation if you've got an interesting new outfit you're saving to wear while you're away – or maybe it's something that looks too brash at home, but which is just right with a tan on a sultry summer evening. Here's an ideal chance for you to show your creativity in embroidery. Buy a plain garment cheaply from a chain store, and add an embroidery of your own design to personalize it. Do the same for the children; make them something special for the holidays by embroidering a holiday motif or border on to an ordinary pair of shorts or a plain T-shirt.

Holidays are good chances to pick up new inspiration and ideas for your embroidery resources file; make sure that you pack a notebook and pencil. Make a note of your ideas, buy postcards and take snapshots which you can translate into ideas for embroideries or new colour schemes for your stitchery projects once you return home.

Buttons come in wonderful shapes, and can inspire their own embroidery. Create your own border down a child's holiday outfit by adding simple embroidered shapes to bright buttons.

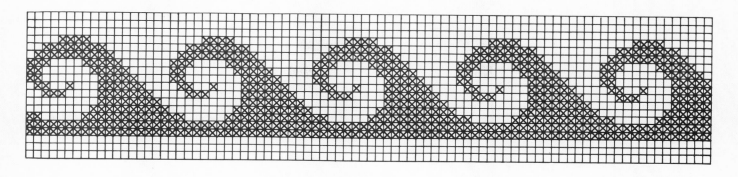

The seashore teems with life – not only aquatic life, represented by fish, shells, starfish and seahorses, but nautical life too. The designs here were all inspired in some way by the seashore, and will be just right for putting you in the holiday mood. The rope and knots border would be ideal as a frame round a nautical embroidery for a sailing enthusiast, perhaps worked in naval shades of blue and gold. The shell and wave borders would look lovely stitched round the hem of a summer skirt, and individual shell motifs could be very dramatic machine appliquéd on to a beach towel.

The pattern of shells opposite would fit well into a cushion shape; you could work it as a needlepoint chart and choose a colour scheme of sea greens and blues or shell pinks and corals; alternatively, work it as a quilted design on glazed cotton, or appliqué it in plain colours and stitch the lines of the shells in pearly threads. You could use the simple boat frieze to decorate a child's bedroom curtains.

Even in these days of television and videos, circuses and fairgrounds can still weave their magic spells in children's hearts, and they have inspired most of the designs on these pages. Music blaring out from fairground rides, the bright diamonds of the harlequin and candy-striped poles on merry-go-round horses; they are all represented here, ready for you to interpret in embroidery. Choose bright, vibrant colours – there's nothing subtle about a fair! Use the clown on the opposite page to stitch a mirror frame for your child's bedroom; instead of putting patterns on to the balls the clown is juggling, you could spell out the child's name in surface embroidery, adding more balls if necessary.

Chapter 9

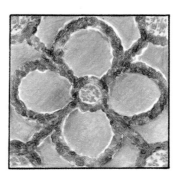

KNOTS AND MAZES

Lines that meander to and fro, in and out, in decorative patterns can provide all kinds of ideas for embroiderers. Knot gardens, mazes or labyrinths, Greek key patterns, Roman mosaic designs, children's puzzles, Celtic stonework, Islamic painted tiles; the lines twist and turn, sometimes predictably, sometimes unexpectedly, producing patterns that are just asking for interpretation in stitchery.

PREVIOUS PAGE Knot gardens – formal gardens laid out in complex shapes – are excellent sources of design inspiration for embroiderers, as you can see from this cross stitch panel.

RIGHT The hooked motifs typical of Persian carpet designs interlink around this needlepoint border.

The sources of inspiration for knots and maze patterns are many and varied, and can be the excuse for very self-indulgent days spent researching in libraries! Illuminated mediaeval manuscripts, especially very early Celtic ones, are rich in intertwining designs; you may find that your library or bookshop has facsimile copies of books such as the Book of Kells, which has some particularly inspiring patterns. Sometimes these twisting designs cover entire pages, known as carpet pages, and you'll often find – if you have the patience – that they are made up of a single interweaving line. The

The technique known as Swiss embroidery has been used on this gingham table mat to produce an interlocking design; the stitches round the white squares transform them cleverly into circles.

single line was one way in which the illuminators tried to express the idea of eternity. You may also be able to track down source books that feature patterns from illuminations, and other Celtic inspirations such as carved crosses, book covers, jewellery and architecture; there has been a vogue in recent years for re-printing books on decorative styles from all eras, and these usually include many pattern and border ideas. It's also worth looking in books and catalogues of Art Nouveau artefacts; there was a great revival of interest in Celtic patterns at the turn of the century, and many designs from that time feature these fascinating intertwining lines.

This piece of machine embroidery was based on an Islamic tile pattern; one interweaving line produces the complex star shape.

The stepped motifs of a Turkish rug inspired this formal pattern; the bronze metallic thread used for one of the lines of cross stitch brings a touch of the East to the design.

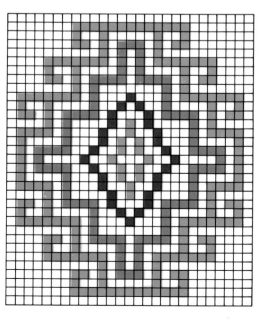

Ancient Greece and Rome also made good use of entwining patterns; you will find examples on pottery and architecture of the time, and particularly in mosaic patterns from the ancient Roman world. The so-called Greek key pattern is famous for its variations, which are found on everything from floors to woven textiles, but it is also found in many places outside Greece, particularly in the decorative designs of China. Regular patterns or straight lines like the Greek key adapt very well to counted thread techniques; once you have worked out a chart for one section of the design, you can repeat it as often as necessary.

Little square knot designs form the motif for these needlepoint bookmarks worked in two colourways on plastic canvas. Extend the basic pattern to make a border for a cross stitch skirt or peasant blouse.

Islamic art features some spectacular interwoven designs; browse through books on North African and Middle Eastern countries, and you will find patterns of breath-taking complexity in their tiles and stonework, as well as simpler designs that are not so daunting to convert to embroidery ideas. Think through different techniques you can use to interpret the designs at different scales, from tiny counted thread patterns to full-scale patchwork quilts.

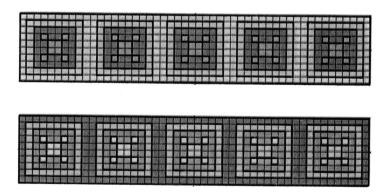

Celtic designs are constant sources of inspiration for the embroiderer, as the designs here show. Some of the patterns are traditional quilting borders, and all of these ideas would look good interpreted in wadded quilting, but they also lend themselves very well to Italian, or corded quilting, where cords are threaded through stitched channels. You could work several of the motif designs in the centre of a bed quilt or sofa quilt, and extend one of the borders to the right dimensions to go around the edges; several of the more complex border designs include a section for working round a corner. Many of these patterns would also look effective worked in shadow quilting, with muted colours coming through a sheer top fabric.

You don't need to stop at quilting, either; all of the designs can be worked in traditional and contemporary embroidery methods, and if you use an acetate grid, it is easy to translate the patterns into charts for counted thread embroidery techniques. The five-pointed star would fit well in the centre of a cushion, perhaps worked in needlepoint or cross stitch.

In contrast to many of the smoothly flowing Celtic designs, interweaving designs from further East are often based on geometric shapes. Many Islamic patterns tend to be formed of networks of straight lines at set angles, built up into complex starburst shapes, although they do incorporate curves occasionally. Greek designs tend towards the geometric too; I've included two variations of the ever-popular Greek key pattern, one as a square design and one as a border. The geometry behind designs like this make them very easy to translate into techniques such as cross stitch, drawn thread work, needlepoint etc, but there are plenty of ways of using the designs for surface embroidery too.

Chapter 10

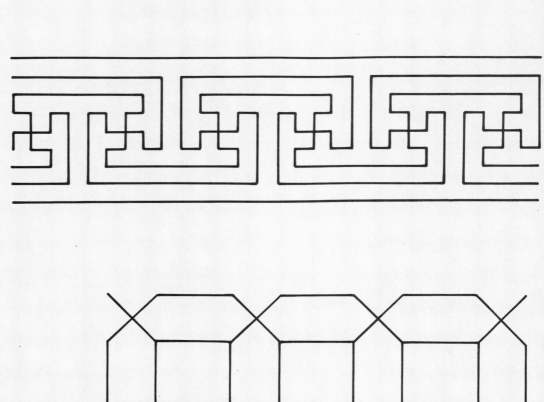

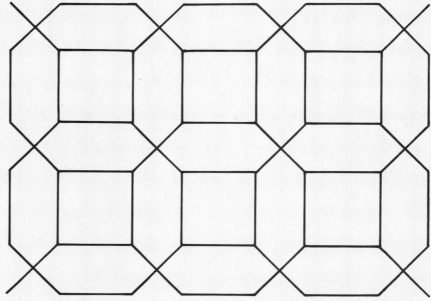

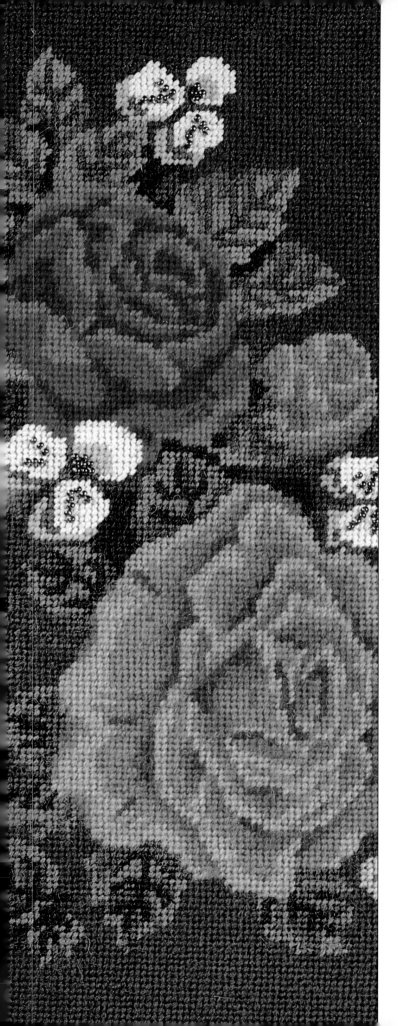

SPECIAL OCCASIONS

Everyone enjoys a celebration, whether it's a wedding, a birth, an anniversary, a house-warming, or a birthday. Special occasions are something to look forward to before they happen, something to enjoy during the day, and something to look back on for many years afterwards. Use the designs in this section to create lasting mementoes of important occasions for your family and friends.

PREVIOUS PAGE Roses are often associated with special occasions, and can be interpreted in many different ways. The needlepoint panel here uses a realistic depiction of roses in traditional colours.

Inspiration for special occasion embroideries can spring from all kinds of places. It's relatively easy to collect ideas for use on wedding embroideries – weddings are excuses for all kinds of one-off items, and if you invest in several of the large bridal magazines, or pick up some brochures from firms that provide clothes and services for weddings, you will probably find enough ideas to stimulate your own embroidery designs for years!

Initials, names and dates are always popular, too, and make a present really personal to the couple; look in the library or in lettering books for good well-formed alphabets and numerals, and if you are working with initials, try various arrangements until you have found a good way of combining them. If you're feeling adventurous, you could try designing your own monogram for the couple, with the letters intertwining in traditional fashion.

RIGHT Stitch a cross stitch frame of ribbons and hearts for the perfect wedding picture. The frame itself would make a lovely and unusual wedding present, and is a good design for wedding anniversaries too.

Birthdays and anniversaries are a bit harder to design for. As with weddings, names or initials can be a good starting point, but you don't want to repeat the same idea year after year. The number of the birthday or anniversary is another source of inspiration – you can always choose a favourite motif, and stitch it an appropriate number of times on a card or sampler, or simply do large numerals that you can then fill in decoratively. Have a look at birthday cards and wrapping papers for inspiration, then work up your own design from any interesting ideas you see.

ABOVE Here a simple border has been stitched on to a wedding veil with shadow-work bows and beads. The pattern is echoed in a single bow motif stitched on to a prayer book in satin stitch and outlined in gold.

LEFT An embroidered heart is a lovely way to say 'I love you', as you can see from this decorative needlepoint example.

Weddings are an ideal opportunity to create a unique work of art. An embroidery will be a touching example of your love for the couple, as well as being a very personal present; if you tie it in with their wedding day as well, it will be a reminder of a happy day.

Flowers are always associated with weddings, so several of these designs feature flowers in different forms. Use the bouquet design small on a card, or larger on a picture or a cushion – if the couple want, you could even make a ring-cushion for them to use during the service. Attach the rings with two tiny ribbon bows. To make the design extra-special you could stitch it in colours that match the colours of the flowers for the wedding. The forget-me-not bow makes a very pretty card design, or alternatively, this or the lily design would look lovely stitched on to a wedding dress or veil.

A photograph frame for a favourite wedding picture is a present that is both pretty and practical. Stitch the frame with the ribbon border in white-on-white, or choose colours that tone with the colours of the wedding, perhaps the flowers or the bridesmaids' dresses. For a bolder effect, stitch the frame using the wild strawberry design in white, red and shades of green.

Birthdays and special anniversaries are often occasions for big celebrations, and you'll find these designs useful if you want to stitch an embroidery to help celebrate. You might want to use one of the designs that captures the vital number of years in stitchery; you can always combine the border from one design with the numbers shown on another, for instance, if you want the number 25 in the heart-shaped frame. With the little candles, you can extend or contract the number to suit the occasion, so you could use this basic design for anything from a birthday card for a small child to a retirement card for 50 years' service – if you've got the patience to stitch that many candles! The scrolls opposite are particularly useful for more formal designs, for instance, if you want to embroider a present for a graduation.

Weddings, anniversaries, St Valentine's Day, or simply a unique present for the love of your life: hearts are perennial favourites as motifs for decorating items to celebrate special occasions. All the designs here feature hearts in different styles, from the racy heart bow to the more formal counted thread border. You can make the colour schemes bold and brash, using red and other primaries, or softer and more subtle. Also, you can make the designs as simple or complicated as you want – your heart embroidery could be anything from a single cross-stitch heart on a tiny card to a full-size appliqué quilt based on the heart lattice design. The stained glass heart opposite produces totally different effects depending on the colours and materials used; for a pretty Victorian look stitch it in shades of pink and add ribbons and lace, or re-create it in brilliant jewel colours edged with black on a cushion stitched in needlepoint.

Chapter 11

CHRISTMAS

Many of us feel that Christmas has become too commercialized – Father Christmas appears in every large store, carols are played over every public address system, and in the rush to make sure that we remember presents for everyone and that the turkey is big enough, we forget what Christmas really means. In this section I've included designs that hark back to more traditional Christmases; the star hovers over the stable, candle-light glows in the darkness, and angels trumpet out the good news of Jesus' birth.

PREVIOUS PAGE A ring of angels makes a pretty centrepiece for a Christmas tablecloth with stars, bells and holly.

BELOW This glittering angel sits in a frame of gold and sky colours.

Christmas is an ideal opportunity for decorating the house, and getting out old familiar decorations to put on the tree or over the mantelpiece is part of the pre-Christmas ritual in many families. It's a good idea to add to those decorations year by year, and to produce some new pieces that will become part of the tradition. You could try making one new decoration each year for the tree – hand-stitched designs always look pretty among the baubles – or produce table linen, wall hangings, pictures, cards and other one-off items to bring the Christmas spirit to your house. You could even stitch a lasting advent calendar to help your children pass the exciting days until Christmas!

Keep your Christmas tree needles off the carpet with this tree mat, decorated with a border of parcels worked in large cross stitch. The mat will show off your presents, too!

This seasonal table runner uses cross stitch in Christmas colours of red, green and gold for a festive and traditional look.

The cross stitch border on this Christmas buffet cloth couldn't be simpler, but it will add a personal touch to any Christmas meal, formal or informal.

It's worth making a collection of inspirational ideas for your own Christmas designs. Christmas cards often carry stylized motifs, so go through your cards when you take them down, and save any which look as though they could be starting points for your own designs. The same is true of wrapping paper, printed ribbons, and Christmas issues of magazines; go through them after Christmas, and tear or cut out sections that might prove useful. The words of Christmas carols can be good starting points for designs, and if you look for books on the seasonal traditions of other countries, it can broaden your ideas beyond the

obvious. Green and red, silver and gold are traditional colour schemes for Christmas stitchery, but other royal colours like crimson, purple, jade green and royal blue also look very effective. Experiment with some of the metallic threads that are available for both hand and machine embroidery – they add opulence to your designs and glisten beautifully under the Christmas tree lights and candles.

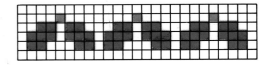

Bright felt stockings in seasonal colours are quickly embroidered with simple patterns and make cheerful Christmas tree decorations; stuff them with sweets, tinsel or little presents.

It's always fun to make the table look special for Christmas Day, and one way of doing that is to embroider a set of seasonal table linen. You could use the cracker or Christmas tree borders shown here around a tablecloth or on table mats and napkins, and both designs would also look good round a cloth under the Christmas tree. Make your own Christmas cards or pictures, or a Christmas mobile, with the bow, the angels or the doves. The candles could be used for the edges of a large mat for the centre of the table; increase or reduce the number of candles to fit.

Christmas wreaths always look welcoming; you could stitch the one opposite in appliqué shapes or large cross stitch and hang it on the wall or use it as the centrepiece for the dining table on Christmas Day. The shapes in the border below are very versatile; cut them out from coloured felt and appliqué them to a Christmas stocking, or round the edges of a tree cloth or tablecloth. You could also use them to stitch individual decorations for the tree, or put them on to the front of little pockets on a fabric advent calendar — each pocket could contain a sweet or other treat.

The star border would look striking round the edge of a Christmas embroidery or crib scene; stitch the stars in gold, silver and bronze metallic thread to make them sparkle, and use a dark background fabric, such as midnight blue satin, to suggest a wintry night.

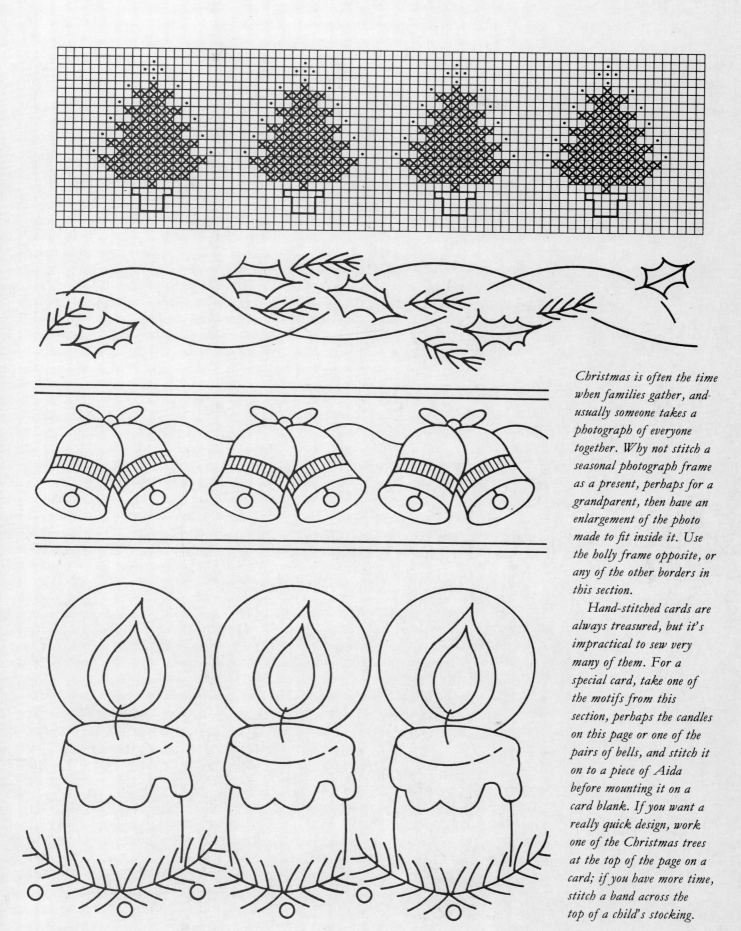

Christmas is often the time when families gather, and usually someone takes a photograph of everyone together. Why not stitch a seasonal photograph frame as a present, perhaps for a grandparent, then have an enlargement of the photo made to fit inside it. Use the holly frame opposite, or any of the other borders in this section.

Hand-stitched cards are always treasured, but it's impractical to sew very many of them. For a special card, take one of the motifs from this section, perhaps the candles on this page or one of the pairs of bells, and stitch it on to a piece of Aida before mounting it on a card blank. If you want a really quick design, work one of the Christmas trees at the top of the page on a card; if you have more time, stitch a band across the top of a child's stocking.

129

MATERIALS, TECHNIQUES AND STITCHES

PLANNING YOUR EMBROIDERY

Before you embark on any piece of embroidery, whether in free stitching, counted thread work, appliqué or quilting, take time to do some basic planning. Think about the feeling you are trying to create in your design and the use to which your work will be put. Then look at all the possible colours, fabrics and stitches you could use to achieve this.

This stage is always the most enjoyable for me: researching, planning alternatives and developing ideas before deciding on the final interpretation. My advice would be to follow your own instincts for each of your embroideries. In this way you will build on your own preferences and strengths, and gain in understanding with each piece of work you do.

The following guide-lines will help you with your planning and familiarize you with some of the materials, techniques and stitches you can use.

MATERIALS

THREADS There are many different types of embroidery thread in a huge range of colours, so do experiment with them instead of playing safe with just one or two familiar ones. Shiny threads include pearl cotton, coton à broder, pure silk and stranded cotton. The latter is very versatile as it can be split up into separate strands and recombined to make different thicknesses. Different shades can be mixed in this way for subtle effects.

Soft embroidery cotton is a matt thread, slightly thicker than stranded cotton. There are also some beautiful metallic threads to add sparkle to your embroidery. Woollen yarns include tapestry wool, Persian wool and crewel wool, and textured knitting wool can often give interesting effects for a change.

FABRICS Free-style embroidery can be worked on all kinds of fabric, depending on the effect you want to achieve. Cotton and linen are ideal for garments or household items, providing an excellent base for embroidery. Silk is wonderful to work with and very luxurious. Oddments of dress or furnishing fabrics can make interesting backgrounds, and calico, being inexpensive, is useful for experimenting with different stitches.

For cross stitch work, you will need evenweave fabric with easily countable threads, while, for needlepoint, canvas is available in a range of mesh sizes.

NOTIONS You can make use of some of the notions available from haberdashery departments or craft shops to add interest to your embroidery. Beads, sequins, buttons, ribbons, lace, cord and braid can all be incorporated into a design to great effect, giving it texture and detail.

These exquisite designs are worked as borders on nineteenth-century Turkish hand-towels made of cotton or linen.

The rows of patterning on this picture make use of ribbons and beads as well as embroidery threads. The canvas shows through in some areas to give extra texture to the design.

FABRIC PAINTS AND CRAYONS These add an extra dimension to an embroidery and are used by many designers to create subtle effects in their work. A painted fabric background can provide a coloured base for embroidery stitches which would be difficult to achieve in any other way.

There are paints and crayons available for use on both natural and synthetic fabrics. Depending on the type, these fabric colours can be applied with a brush, stencilled or sprayed on to fabric, or a design can be drawn on to paper and then transferred to the fabric by ironing.

EQUIPMENT

NEEDLES It is important to choose the correct type and size of needle for your work. Crewel needles have a long eye which will take various thicknesses of thread. Sharps are shorter with a smaller eye, suitable for only one or two strands of stranded cotton or for sewing thread. Betweens are short, sharp needles used in quilting. Tapestry needles are blunt and so do not split the threads of the fabric. They are used for needlepoint and cross stitch.

SCISSORS You will need a good pair of sharp pointed embroidery scissors for cutting threads and a pair of dressmaking shears for cutting fabric.

FRAMES Although some people prefer not to use a frame, it is important for many types of embroidery to work on stretched fabric. Both round and rectangular frames can be mounted on stands, leaving both hands free for stitching.

Ring frames are suitable for small areas of work and come in a range of diameters. It is a good idea to wrap a strip of thin fabric around the inner ring to protect the fabric on which you are working. Remember to remove your embroidery from the ring at the end of each work session, so as not to mark the fabric.

Mount larger pieces of work and needlepoint canvas on to a rectangular slate or rotating frame, or, alternatively, use artist's stretchers or even an old picture frame, attaching the fabric with drawing pins or staples.

TRACING THE DESIGN

Using a pencil, trace your chosen motifs from the book on to tracing paper. Then place the tracing paper on to a white background and sharpen up any lines which are not quite clear. Go over the entire design in black ink to give you good strong guide-lines.

At this stage, enlarge or reduce your motifs if you need to. You could do this by drawing a grid over your design and then copying it on to a larger or smaller grid. Alternatively, simply use a photocopier to enlarge or reduce it in size.

Also at this stage, you could digress into experimenting with colourways. Take advantage of technology again and make several photocopies of your design on which you can then try out colour ideas with felt tip pens or watercolours. If you have already decided on a colour scheme for your embroidery, match the thread colours on your photocopy to make sure they really do work together.

You can use your coloured copy to pin on to the background fabric to see the effectiveness of your idea, but remember to transfer the design from a clear black-and-white copy.

TRANSFERRING THE DESIGN TO FABRIC

There are several ways of transferring your design on to the fabric.

1. Place dressmaker's carbon paper face down on the fabric with your tracing on top. Then go over the lines with a sharp pencil. The carbon image will appear on the fabric.

2. Pin the tracing (or tissue) paper to the fabric and baste around all the lines with small stitches. Then score around the lines with a needle and pull the paper away to leave the tacked outline.

3. With a light fabric, tape your tracing to a clean white surface with the fabric over the top. Draw the lines, which will show through from the tracing, on to the fabric with a sharp hard crayon in an appropriate colour. If the tracing does not show through very clearly, it may help to tape it to a well-lit window instead.

You can use this method for transferring designs on to canvas, too, using an indelible marking pen. In this way, you can work the trace patterns in the book as needlepoint designs as well as in free-style embroidery. You simply fill in the traced outlines with your chosen needlepoint stitches instead of having to follow a chart.

4. 'Prick and pounce' is a traditional method suitable for more intricate designs. With this method, you prick little holes all around the design outlines with a crewel needle. Then tape the tracing over the fabric on a board and, with a small felt pad, rub talc (for dark fabrics) or talc mixed with powdered charcoal (for light fabrics) through the holes. Join the dots with a fine line of watercolour paint.

USING A CHART

Needlepoint and cross stitch designs are usually worked by following a chart. Each square on the chart equals a needlepoint stitch or a cross stitch, which is worked on canvas or even-weave fabric.

Remember that the size of the mesh plays an important part in the size of the finished embroidery. A pattern worked on a 10-gauge canvas, for example, will be much bigger than the same pattern worked on 18-gauge canvas.

FINISHING OFF

If your embroidery needs pressing, place it face down on a thick towel or blanket covered with a clean white cloth. Cover the back of the embroidery with another cloth, then gently steam press from the back so that the stitches are not flattened.

Needlepoint may need to be stretched back into shape after it is finished. Dampen the needlepoint and place it face down on to several layers of blotting paper on a clean wooden board. Working from the centre outwards, stretch one edge at a time, pinning with rustproof drawing pins into the board. When the needlepoint is 'square', leave it to dry completely (which may take several days), then remove it from the board.

MOUNTING EMBROIDERY

If you would like to mount your work as a panel, a simple way is to stretch it over stiff card or hardboard. Make sure you leave a good border of fabric around your embroidery for turnings. Place the embroidery face down with the card, cut to the correct size, on top. Turn over the excess fabric and begin lacing from side to side with strong thread, starting at the centre of each side and working outwards each time. Repeat this process from top to bottom.

TECHNIQUES AND STITCHES

APPLIQUÉ Many of the designs in this book can be worked completely or partially in appliqué. Combining appliqué with embroidery will bring you some exciting effects, adding texture and areas of solid colour.

A shadow work border is very effective on the translucent fabric of a half-curtain.

With fabrics that tend to fray, make a small turning all around the edge of the shape and stitch to the base fabric with slipstitch. Curves will need to be clipped first. Other, firmer fabrics can be attached with buttonhole or blanket stitch or, for speed, machine zigzag stitch.

QUILTING Motifs with a fairly simple outline can look very effective worked in quilting, and you can then use them to decorate padded items such as winter jackets or cot quilts. Padded quilting is worked through three layers of fabric — the top fabric, the wadding itself and the backing fabric. Synthetic wadding is available in a variety of thicknesses.

Once the motif is marked on to the top fabric, the layers need to be tacked firmly together, either in a grid formation or in lines radiating out from the centre. Then the design can be worked in small neat running stitches or alternatively in back stitch for a more pronounced outline.

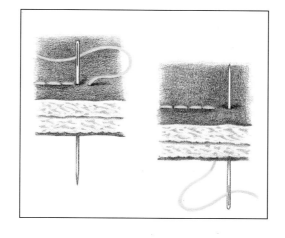

The padded effect in quilting is provided by a layer of wadding sandwiched between two layers of fabric. Running stitch or back stitch as shown here are used to outline the design.

USING WASTE CANVAS You may decide to work a cross stitch motif on to fabric which is too fine for the threads to be counted, for example, a flower sprig on a fine cotton blouse or a denim jacket. You can do this by working the stitches over 'waste' canvas which is made specially for this purpose. Tack it to the fabric, stitch the design and, when the motif is complete, dampen the embroidery so that the canvas threads can be withdrawn one by one, leaving the design on the fabric.

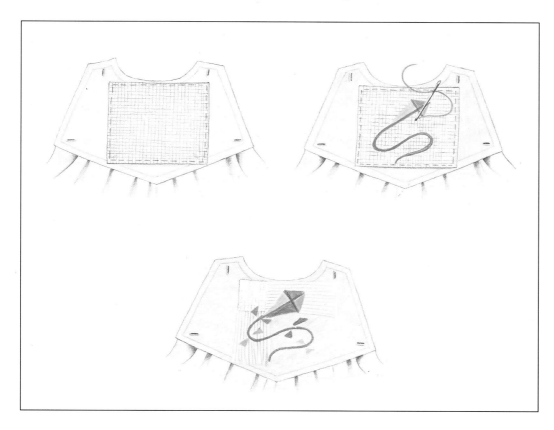

When using waste canvas, tack it to the fabric, work the cross stitch design over it and then withdraw the dampened canvas threads.

STITCH LIBRARY

FREE-STYLE STITCHES

STRAIGHT STITCH These are single stitches which can be worked in a regular fashion or just scattered at random. They can vary in length but should not be made too loose or long in case they snag.

SATIN STITCH This consists of straight stitches worked closely side by side across a shape. They can be upright or slanting, and may be padded slightly by working running stitch underneath. Satin stitch makes a beautiful smooth surface, and if shiny threads are used, reflects the light in an effective way.

LONG-AND-SHORT STITCH Beautiful shaded effects can be achieved with this stitch. It is very useful for filling shapes which are too big to be covered by satin stitch. Work the first row with alternate long and short stitches, following the outline of the shape. Fill in the following rows with stitches of similar lengths, keeping the embroidery smooth.

SEEDING This is a simple but useful filling stitch which gives a speckled effect. It is made up of short straight stitches scattered randomly over the fabric within a shape. For a varying density of tone, the stitches can be closely grouped in one area and spaced further apart in another.

SHEAF STITCH This filling stitch can be worked in staggered rows as shown or in horizontal rows with all the bundles of stitches in line with each other. Make three vertical satin stitches and tie them in the middle with two overcasting stitches. Then insert the needle into the fabric to move on to the next stitch group.

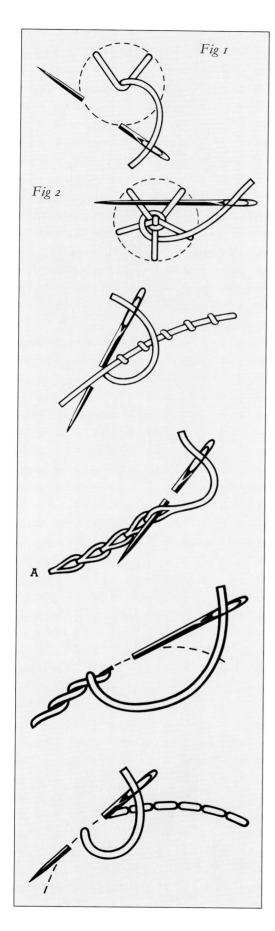

Fig 1

Fig 2

SPIDER'S WEB FILLING First make spokes around the circle as follows. Start with a fly stitch with a long tail, then work two straight stitches into the centre on either side of the tail (*fig. 1*). Weave the thread under and over the spokes to fill the circle (*fig. 2*).

COUCHING Lay a thread along the line of the motif. Then tie it down at regular intervals with another thread, using a contrasting colour or weight if required for effect.

SPLIT STITCH This is an outline stitch, but also works as a filling stitch where rows side by side make a fine flat surface. Bring the needle out at A, then take a small back stitch, piercing the thread with the needle tip as you pull it through.

STEM STITCH This is an ideal stitch for flower stems and outlines, but can also be arranged in rows side by side to fill in shapes. Working from left to right, make small even stitches along the outline, overlapping each stitch with the previous one as shown.

BACK STITCH A basic outline stitch, this can also be used in quilting instead of running stitch where a more defined line is required. Bring the needle through on the stitching line, take a small backward stitch and bring the needle out again a little further along. Take another backward stitch into the same hole as the previous stitch and so on.

CABLE STITCH Work cable stitch from left to right. Bring the needle through on the design line. Keeping thread below needle, insert the needle from right to left as in *fig. 1*. Work the next stitch in the same way, but this time keep the thread above the needle (*fig. 2*).

FRENCH KNOTS Bring the thread through and, holding it down with your left thumb, twist the needle around it twice as shown in *fig. 1*. Keeping the thread taut, insert the needle back into the fabric where it first came out, as shown by the arrow. Pull the thread through and bring to the front again for the next French knot (*fig. 2*).

BULLION KNOTS Make a back stitch the length you wish the bullion knot to be, bringing just the needle point back through at the beginning of the stitch. Twist the thread around the needle so that it equals the length of the back stitch. Keeping the thread taut, pull the needle through and take it back to the beginning of the stitch (see arrow).

CORAL STITCH The knots in coral stitch can be spaced closely or further apart. Start at the right of the design. Lay the thread along the line, holding it down with your thumb. Make a tiny stitch under the line and, with thread under needle, draw through and pull up gently to form a knot.

BLANKET STITCH Blanket stitch (or buttonhole stitch if closed up) is useful for working around appliqué shapes. Bring the thread through on the lower line, make a stitch from the upper to the lower line and, with the thread under the needle, pull the stitch through.

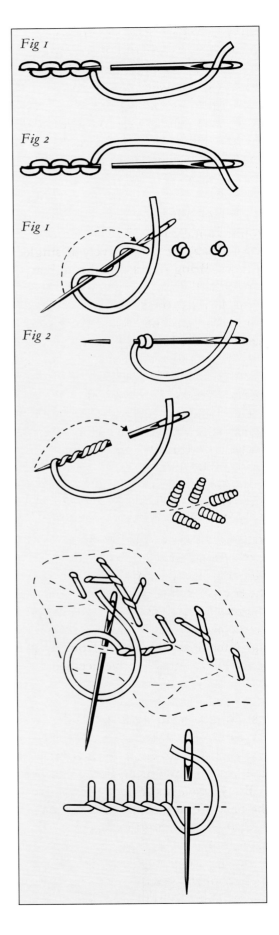

FEATHER STITCH Bring the thread through at the top centre. Insert the needle to the right and make a stitch downwards towards the centre, keeping the thread under the needle. Next, insert the needle to the left and make another stitch downwards and towards the centre with the thread under the needle.

FLY STITCH Fly stitch may be worked in horizontal rows (*fig. 1*) or vertical rows (*fig. 2*), or alternatively as single stitches. Bring the needle through at top left and insert it again to the right, holding the thread down with your thumb. Make a small tying stitch to anchor the loop, as shown.

CRETAN STITCH Start centrally on the left of the shape. Take a small stitch from the lower line towards the centre with thread under needle (*fig. 1*). Then take a stitch from the upper line in the same way, with thread under needle (*fig. 2*).

HERRINGBONE STITCH Bring the thread through at the bottom. Moving slightly to the right, insert the needle from right to left along the top line and pull through, with thread below needle. Again moving to the right, make another stitch from right to left, with thread above needle.

FISHBONE STITCH *Fig. 1* shows the closed version of the stitch. Make a small stitch from A along the centre line of the motif. Bring the thread out at B and make a slanting stitch across the base of the first stitch. Come out at C, then make another slanting stitch across the base of the previous stitch and so on. *Fig. 2* shows the open version of the stitch. Bring the thread out at A and follow in sequence.

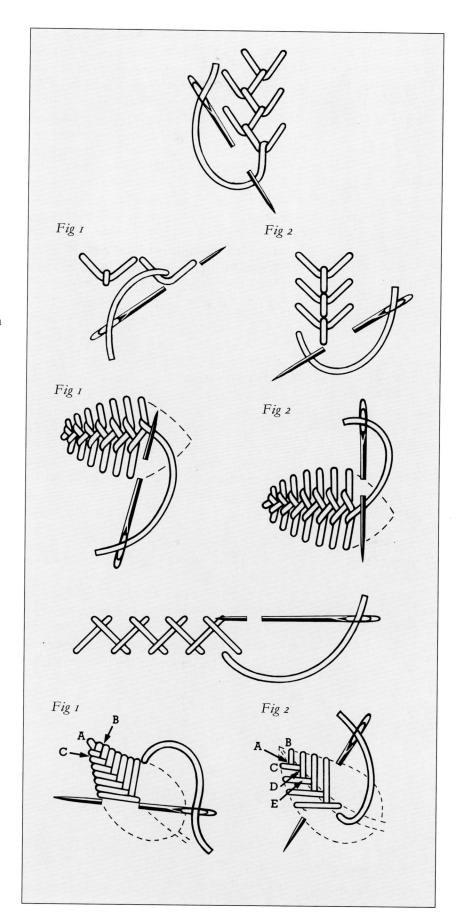

Fig 1   *Fig 2*

Fig 1   *Fig 2*

Fig 1   *Fig 2*

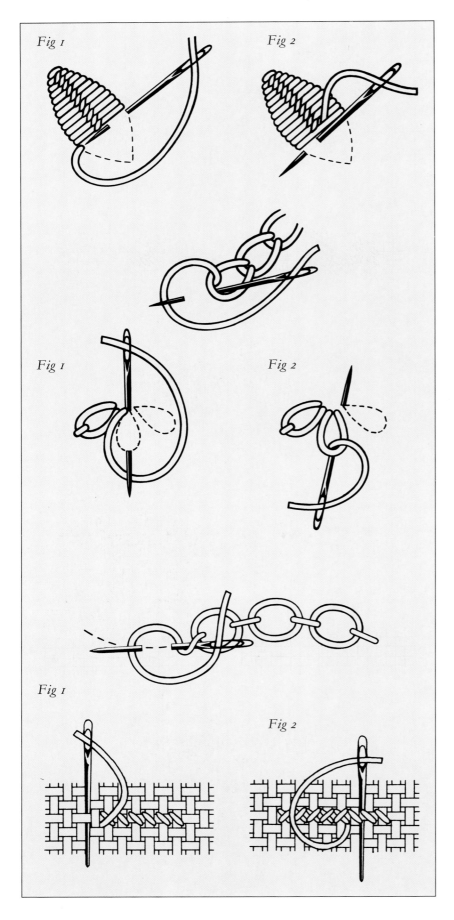

ROUMANIAN STITCH Bring the thread out at the left of the motif, take it to the right and make a stitch to the centre with thread below needle (*fig. 1*). Take another stitch from centre to left with the thread above the needle (*fig. 2*). This makes a small tying stitch as shown.

CHAIN STITCH Chain stitch can be used as a filling stitch if worked in adjacent rows or as a spiral. It is also an outline stitch. Bring the thread through at the top of the line. Reinsert the needle in the same place and, holding down the loop with your thumb, bring the needle out a short way down. Pull the thread through to form a chain.

DETACHED CHAIN STITCH This is worked in the same way as chain stitch (*fig. 1*), but each loop is anchored down with a small stitch (*fig. 2*). The stitches can be worked singly, grouped into flower petals or scattered over the fabric like seeding.

CABLE CHAIN STITCH Bring the needle through at right. Holding the thread down with your left thumb, twist the needle round the thread as shown. Make a loop, hold it down with your thumb and take a stitch with thread under needle. This makes alternate chain stitches and linking stitches.

COUNTED THREAD

CROSS STITCH The crosses are worked in two stages. First work a row of half cross stitch from right to left (*fig. 1*), then work back the other way to complete the crosses (*fig. 2*). The top arm of each cross stitch should slope in the same direction.

NEEDLEPOINT STITCHES

TENT STITCH Tent stitch can be worked either in diagonal rows as in *figs. 1 and 2* or in horizontal rows as in *figs. 3 and 4*. The former method is preferable, where possible, as it prevents the canvas from being distorted by the stitching.

HALF CROSS STITCH This needlepoint stitch resembles tent stitch but is worked differently. It is useful when embroidering with a thick yarn, as it is not as bulky. Each diagonal stitch is worked over one canvas intersection and the stitches on the back are vertical.

BRICK STITCH This consists of vertical stitches worked in staggered rows. In *fig. 1* long and short stitches are worked alternately. In *fig. 2*, the next and all subsequent rows interlock neatly with the one above.

HUNGARIAN STITCH This consists of interlocking rows of a small diamond pattern and is very effective worked in more than one colour. The vertical straight stitches are worked in groups over two, four and two canvas threads respectively, leaving two canvas threads between each group. Each row fits into the previous one.

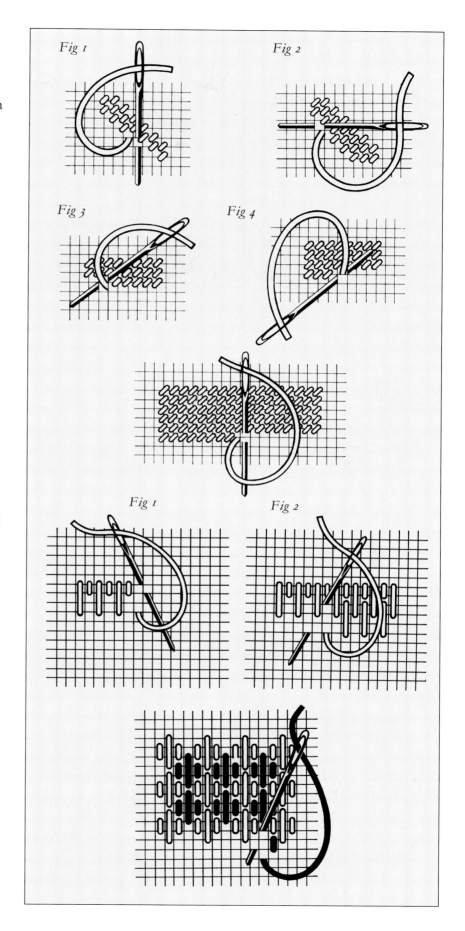

Fig 1   Fig 2

Fig 3   Fig 4

Fig 1   Fig 2

INDEX

ACKNOWLEDGMENTS

The publishers would like to acknowledge the following embroidery designers whose work is reproduced in this book.

Amanda Burton Wright 34–5, 36 below; Coats Design Studio 91; Stella Edwards 22 above and below, 26, 37 below, 49, 60, 61, 70, 71, 101, 111; Anna Griffiths 13, 27, 38, 48, 98 below, 109 above, 123, 132; Caroline Kelley 90, 109 below; Caroline Kelley for BEST magazine 80, 81; Gail Lawther book jacket, 11 below, 12, 39, 69, 82, 83, 99, 100, 108, 121 above, 122, 134; Susan Lethbridge 5, 78–9; Judith Newell Price 36 above; Audrey Ormrod 3, 58, 96–7; Permin of Copenhagen, 28 Egegårdsvej, PO Box 4, DK 2610 Rødovre, Copenhagen, Denmark 118–9, 121; Beth Russell for Designers' Forum 25; Sally Saunders 23; Vanessa Stone 37 above, 66–7, 68 below; Molly Verity 2, 24, 59, 88–9, 120; Sarah Windrum/The Arthouse (for Ehrman) 7, 11 above, 68 above, 98 above; Annette Woollard for Applegate Designs 20–1, 56–7, 106–7.

The photographs on the following pages are reproduced with the permission of:

The Board of Trustees of The Victoria and Albert Museum 44–5; The Embroiderers' Guild Collection (photographer Julia Hedgecoe) 8–9, 10, 131; Susie Martin 11 above, 98 above; Freda Parker 23, 46, 47.

The author and publisher have made every effort to trace the copyright holders of the photographs reproduced in this book. If any omissions have occurred, the publisher will be pleased to rectify this in any future reprints.

⚓ Anchor

Coats Crafts internationally market a comprehensive and diverse range of handicraft threads and accessories. The trade mark Anchor represents a wide choice of top quality products for all types of embroidery, tapestry and crochet.
Details of Anchor suppliers are available from:

ENGLAND
Coats Patons Crafts
P. O. Box
McMullen Road
Darlington DL1 1YQ
tel. 0325–381010
fax 0325–382300

DENMARK
Coats Mölnlycke Sytrad A/S
Industrilvaenget 5–9
Lind
DK-7400 Merning
tel. 45 97220800
fax 45 97213957

BELGIUM
Filature et Filteries Réunies N.V.
Burgemeester De Cocklaan 4
B-9320
Erembodegem-Aalst
tel. 053–781108
fax 053–780604

AUSTRIA
Harlander Prym Vertriebsgesellschaft m.b.H.
Autokaderstraße 31
P. O. Box 74
A-1211 Vienna 21
tel. 0222–27716
fax 0222–27716228
tx 114074 HPVG A

GERMANY
Mez AG
Kaisterstraße 1
Postfach 1179
D-7832 Kenzingen
tel. 07644–8020
fax 07644–802252
tx 7722608 MEZ D

NETHERLANDS
Carp-Prym B.V.
Vossenbeemd 104
P. O. Box 11
NL-5700 AA Helmond
tel. 04920–33845
fax 04920–46635
tx 51212 CARPY NL

ITALY
Cucirini Cantoni Coats S.p.A.
Viale F. Restelli, 3/7
I-20124 Milano
tel. 02–69921
fax 02–2844140
tx 332081 CCC I

NORWAY
Coats Multicem A/S
P. B. 1153
N-5001 Bergen
tel. 47 5298110
fax 47 5297704
tx 291820

SPAIN
Coats Fabra
Sant Adriá 20
08030 Barcelona
tel. 93–311.00.11
fax 93–346.49.10
tx 52896 Facoa E

FRANCE
Coats Sartel Loisirs
22, rue de la Tannerie
B. P.
59392 Wattrelos Cedex
tel. 20 75 88 40
fax 20 81 14 67
tx 130 805

SWEDEN
Opti-Nord AB
Box 245
Källbäcksrydsgatan 8
S-501 05 Boras
tel. 46 33157020
fax 46 33158613
tx 36409 S

FINLAND
Opti-Kiito OY
Maukaritie 5
SF-04420 Kerava 2
tel. 358 0244401
fax 358 0246186
tx 121527 Kiito SF